Developing Skill 2

A Guide to 3v3 Soccer Coaching

Peter Prickett

DARK
RIVER

Published in 2019 by Dark River, an imprint of Bennion Kearny Limited.

Copyright © Dark River

Peter Prickett has asserted his right under the Copyright Designs and Patents Act 1988 to be identified as the author of this work

ISBN: 978-1-911121-77-0

Published by Dark River, an imprint of Bennion Kearny Limited
6 Woodside, Churnet View Road, Oakamoor, ST10 3AE

*

Many thanks to Garth Smith for his cover design.

*

BAZOOKAGOAL™

3v3.co.uk

Table of Contents

1

What Do We Love About Football?

I started the first volume of 3v3 with this question. The answer has not changed. It never will.

Competition, glory, drama, storytelling, teamwork, artistry, and skill. As fans, there are two things that we want: victory and entertainment. Sometimes one without the other is not enough. Teams can achieve genuine or relative success yet have an unhappy fan base because they have not been witnessing a style of football that thrills them.

The greatest players are those who provide entertainment and excitement. It may manifest in different ways, but it is near-universal that onlookers will be enraptured by moments of high quality. The higher the quality they see, the higher the entertainment levels rise. This then produces moments that last forever, and keep fans glued to the sport.

We love to debate and discuss. Messi and Ronaldo, who is better? Or who is the greatest? Are either of these players superior to the legends of the past? Pele, Maradona, Cruyff, di Stefano, and any other people brought into the conversation. Each of these players has the quality, skill, decision making, and imagination to execute consistently and in the big moments. These factors, ultimately, are what coaches want for each of their young players.

The aim of the first book (and still the aim of this book) was to help create an environment that releases the inner Messi, Ronaldo, Maradona, at al., of our young footballers.

To my mind, the key is what a player is capable of *with the ball*. The ball and the player need to form a deeply-satisfying long-term relationship – one in which the player has full command of everything that the ball does. The player should be able to demand that the ball momentarily appears to defy physics and behaves in a manner unexpected to their opponent. Immense amounts of practice are required, and many coaches assign time during training to this, but it takes more. Huge numbers of hours spent between a child and a ball are needed to perfect, refine, and experiment things in a quest to find their move.

It all starts with the ability to dribble. A dribble-first mindset. Players need to see an opponent and feel confident that they can take that player on. If they have been brought up as a passer, they will only ever pass when they see an opponent,

Chapter 1

eventually panicking when one comes too close. When a dribbler sees pressure, and an opponent, the mindset is different. This is not to panic; this is opportunity. When they get older, it is easier to teach a player who dribbles too much to pass, than it is to teach a passer to become a dribbler. Tricks and skills are devices to create space and openings; once they are created, players are then judged on the shot, pass, or cross. What is often forgotten is that more players need to have the ability to create those openings in the first place.

Just as the reasons why we love the game have not changed, nor have the reasons for using a 3v3 format. Those reasons begin with 1v1.

If we are going to master the ball, we need to practice using it against an opponent to achieve our dribbling mindset. If we work on ball mastery, and always move straight into situations where it will not be used, then an opportunity is wasted. One versus ones may occur in games where we have overloaded attacking situations, but fast passing outcomes will be far more likely. When playing one versus one – and there is no escaping it – players need to dribble. Players need to face up to, and face off against, other players – both as attackers and defenders. Defending against your immediate opponent is just as important as attacking. If a player cannot defend one on one, they will be picked out. They will be the link in the chain that opponents exploit. It will no longer be 5v5 or 11v11; the game will be 4v5 or 10v11. Not all even match-ups are equal.

If one versus one is so important, why don't we focus on that? Because there is one key decision missing from one versus one. The decision to pass. The absence of this possibility removes a number of actions from the dribbler's arsenal. As well as simply being able to pass, the player is unable to fake to pass. If there are no teammates to pass to, why would a defender believe the action to fake pass? Similarly, if the setup does not involve goals, why would the defender buy a fake shot? We want the player to focus on how to take on an opponent, but the realism eventually needs to be brought in, too.

Any child will tell you that – with three players – a triangle can easily be created. When it comes to passing the football, a triangle is the optimal shape (arguably a diamond is, depending on whether a coach sees a diamond as a diamond, or as two triangles). The player on the ball has two options, immediately creating more possible movements for attackers and more challenges for defenders. An element of choosing a formation can be introduced simply by moving the points of the triangle. Should a team defend with two points closest to their goal or with one? What difference does that make to the opposition? It is the same position for attackers. Do we push two players high and wide or push just one up high acting as a centre-forward? These choices will then affect the actions of the game. In one case, we might see more up, back, and through actions. In another, more overlaps could be possible.

By playing 3v3, players will receive more touches than in 4v4 and 5v5 but fewer than with 1v1 and 2v2. However, they will be able to achieve a greater number of technical and tactical decisions than within the 1v1 and 2v2 environments. Within a 3v3 game, those 1v1 and 2v2 situations will occur with regularity. Not only that, there will be 1v0 situations where a player receives the ball under no pressure. There will be 2v1 attacking overloads, 1v2 defending overloads, 3v1 attacking overloads, 1v3 defending overloads, 3v2 attacking overloads, and 2v3 defending overloads. There will be a greater number of opportunities to dribble but also more decisions as to whether to pass, shoot, or dribble. This is football. The game is fluid, and rarely is it genuinely 11v11. The immediate actions of the game usually take place within a small space. If a photo of an 11v11 match was taken and cropped, the actions in that space would look a lot like a small-sided game. By playing 3v3, we are helping to prepare players for the variable, small moments of the larger game. Since the first book, it would appear that German football is embracing 3v3, with reports suggesting that there are plans to build their next tranche of player development around 3v3. This appears to have prompted debate in England about whether to replace 5v5 with 3v3 as the matchday format for under 7s and under 8s. Whether this actually happens… we will see.

Book one was wonderfully received. I had positive feedback from FA tutors, academy coaches, academics and, most importantly, grassroots coaches. The book was designed to be of practical use, to be returned to with regularity.

Between the release of the first book, and the inception of the second, that was precisely what I did.

During the 2018/19 season, I was fortunate enough to work with two groups of under 8s. One at a development centre for a professional club, the other my local grassroots club. I decided that rather than being a *part of the programme* for these groups, 3v3 would be the *absolute heart* of the sessions.

My reasoning was that, at the very least, the players would come away from sessions having had large amounts of game time, which should leave them happy. Or at least they wouldn't be asking, "When can we have a match?" Interestingly, I did still get asked by certain players, "Can we have a big match?" – and (normally) this came from the physically stronger players, and at the end of the sessions, we would have 6v6 games at the grassroots club. At the development centre, the players rarely asked for a "big match" but we would have them semi-regularly. In the 6v6 games at the grassroots club, the less developed (physically and technically) players would be far less involved and sometimes disengage completely from the larger game. At the development centre, with more equal ability levels, this was less of problem.

Despite the slightly different contexts of the two groups, the method proved to be suitable. Of course, I would be unlikely to advertise any failings to this methodology! It fascinated me to see how the players developed. Not all players showed progress to the same degree, of course. Each player being an individual and on their own developmental path. What did amaze me was that certain players made a quantum leap forward in next to no time. Within three sessions at the grassroots club, one player was displaying previously unseen footwork. At the development centre, one player was producing tricks to beat a player that were not evident during week one. For the 2019/20 season, I have once again taken the under 8s; in week three, a player was showing a previously unseen propensity to take players on using stepovers. I suspect for the impact to be so rapid, it is less related to the method and more related to the mentality. Of course, the mentality is behind the creation of the method, so we cannot completely detach the two.

Building the training format around matches ensured that the players were always involved and always had decisions to make. We deviated from the form within the session to work on aspects of the game, breaking into finishing practices or pressing practices, but never too far from the 3v3 set up to allow for a smooth transition between games and game-based practices. We were still able to work on topics, but the topics were a secondary goal to the philosophy of taking risks and taking players on. It rendered success, or the lack thereof regarding a specific aspect of development, less important. That sidelining of the topic behind a philosophy created a more enjoyable, more playful environment for all involved.

It also meant that players were very keen to return each week.

In May 2019, the two worlds collided. In a rare event, the two teams had the opportunity to play each other at a football festival. I stood on the sideline, watching my two teams face off.

One of the parents looked after the grassroots team while I took the development centre side for the 10-minute game. The only management related to making substitutions halfway through the game. Everything else that came from my mouth or that of the players was positive encouragement: an unusual utopia probably created by the mutual coach connection. The game itself was massively entertaining, with both sets of players producing moments of brilliant skill and imagination. There was one outstanding passing sequence, despite passing never being a real training focus. The foci were intelligence and decision making. Intelligent players will pass, even if this is not an explicit learning outcome.

Footage of the game is available on YouTube
https://www.youtube.com/watch?v=70i24uz7_F0 and you can make up your own minds about whether the players are free to try new things, make decisions, and whether they are enjoying what they are doing.

These worlds would further collide as a few of the grassroots players joined the development centre, though not in the group that I coach.

It was not only with younger age groups that I regularly used the 3v3 sessions. With older groups, I used 3v3 as an arrival activity and a way to build into the main topic. The 3v3 would serve as total free play, initially. Slowly, rules and constraints would be dripped in which served to link the 3v3 exercise into the later focus of the session. Depending on what we were working on, 3v3 formats would also form a portion of the main topic.

During this time, I not only used the sessions of book one, I also generated new session designs and practices which did not make it into that title. Some of the feedback I have had described the first book as comprehensive, yet here was a large amount of material related to 3v3. When reviewing the book, I noted that there were not many practices linked directly to finishing or creating goals. Far from being comprehensive, I had many more avenues to explore.

So, without further ado, please let me present: *Developing Skill 2: A Guide to 3v3 Soccer Coaching.*

2
Warm-up

The objective of the warm-up is to set the theme and tone for the session. We can do this with a small-sided game. Starting the session with a game is great for player engagement, but you may also want to utilise a further activity that enables players to enjoy a large number of ball contacts.

Simplifying the set up for the warm-up exercise will enable a smooth transition from the warm-up into the next phase of the session. My objective is to minimise the amount of equipment required, while incorporating as many football-related actions as possible into the exercises. The exercises in this chapter use no more than eight cones and eight footballs, which should be relatively straightforward to set up and put away quickly, or set up within the area of the main practice.

There are certain core elements players require in order to play. Players need to be able to move. That movement manifests in a number of ways, including purely physical movements such as sprinting and jumping. It also manifests as the movement from position to position in the constant struggle for space. The recognition of space is heavily connected to awareness and observation. Players need to understand where the space is, in order to utilise it. Often players are encouraged to scan and check for space. By deliberately including chaos in practice design, the players are required to 'be aware' in order to have success. It may look like a mess at times, but this is not necessarily a bad thing. Mess and lack of success could be an indicator that we are on the limits of players' capabilities, pushing onto what they will become capable of. The final core element is technical, which can be characterised as passing, dribbling, control, and shooting. If our practices encompass some or all of these elements, we are providing ample opportunities for game-related practice. The same is true of our warm-ups.

The key concept of these exercises is awareness. By increasing the chaos, players will need to be aware of their surroundings and all of the moving parts. The exercises are intended to be multifaceted and game-relevant; being able to remain calm and focused in the face of chaos is highly relevant to the game of football. The notes on the practices are focused on the passing aspects, but there are constant and consistent dribbling elements too. Dribbling through chaos requires the composure and vision alluded to previously.

The final element addressed in these designs is movement, both before and after passing or receiving the ball. The term rotation is used regularly in the notes. In purely football terms, we would most relate rotation to midfield movement, especially in connection with a three-man midfield. However, the practices are not purely designed for football and can easily be applied to futsal (indeed, the principles of invasion games mean that the practices can transfer to basketball, hockey, etc., with relatively few adaptations), where rotation is a vital part of the game. Developing good movement habits in our warm-up phase allows a deeper connection to the other phases.

"I see football as an art, and all players are artists. If you are a top artist, the last thing you would do is paint a picture somebody else has already painted." Cristiano Ronaldo

Kriss-Kross 1

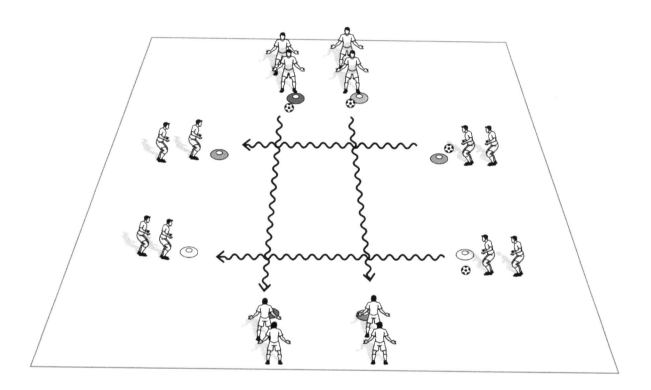

Dribble across the area

- Inside foot only
- Outside foot only
- Sole of the foot only

Add a second ball to the start of each line. Eight footballs are active.

- What tricks can the players use on the way across?
- What are the challenges of the exercise?

Kriss-Kross 2

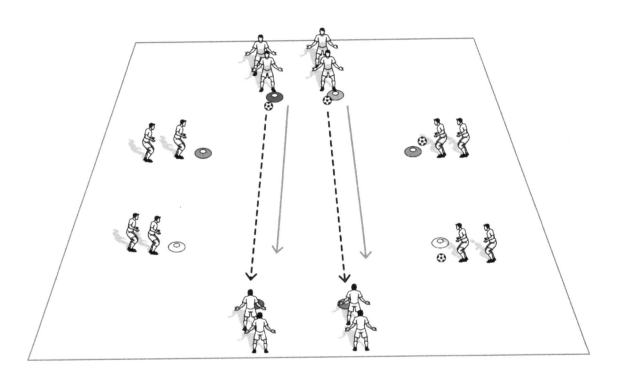

1. Pass across the area
2. Pass and follow across the area

Points

- Timing
- Vision
- Spotting gaps
- Movement away from the cone to receive

Kriss-Kross 3

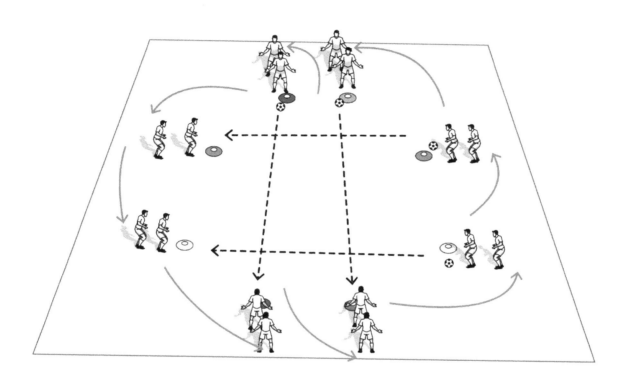

1. Pass across the area, and rotate to your right-hand row after passing
2. Pass across the area, and rotate to your left-hand row after passing

Points

- First touch
- Clean ball strike
- Finding a rhythm/tempo

Kriss-Kross 4

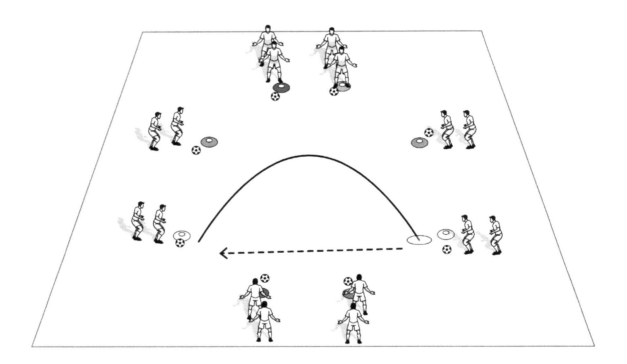

1. Two footballs for each line. One player passes high; the other passes low
2. Still high and low but passing is diagonal (for example, red to yellow)
3. Players rotate to their left after passing high or low

Kriss-Kross 5

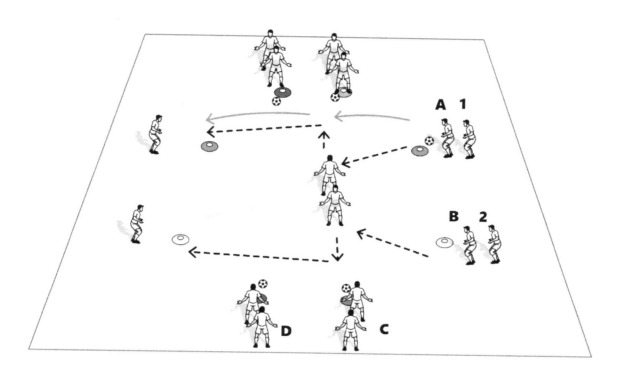

Lines A and B play a one-two across the area using the middle players. The middle players remain in place. Lines D and C dribble across while the other players are passing.

The passers need to find the space around the dribblers. Central players will need to adjust their positions to find space.

Progression – Rotate

The player who passes into the centre follows their pass. The central player passes across to the other side before joining the line of the player who just passed to them.

Kriss-Kross 6

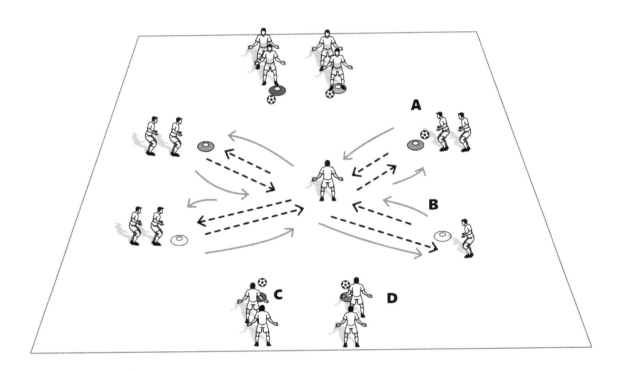

Rotation

Lines A and B pass and follow, with the central player moving out to the wide positions as the wide player takes their place.

Lines C and D dribble across as the passing is occurring.

Kriss-Kross 7

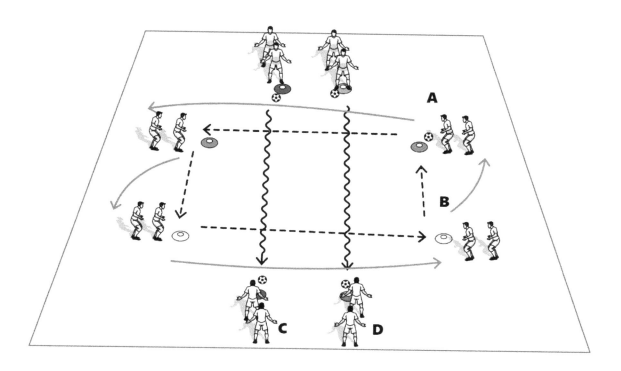

Rotation 2

Lines A and B pass and follow while lines C and D dribble across.

Points

- Touch
- Quality of pass
- Play as quickly as possible
- Awareness

Kriss-Kross 8

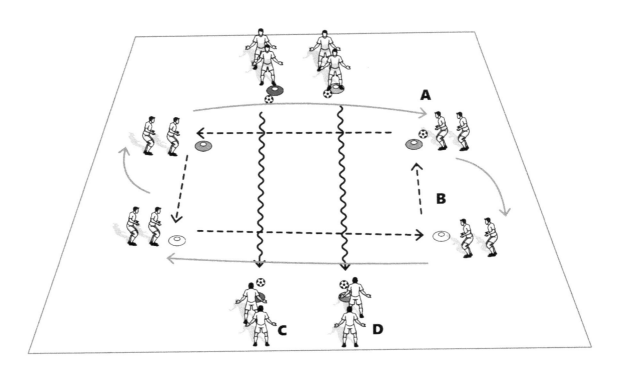

Rotation 3

Lines A and B pass and follow, while lines C and D dribble across.

Reverse movement. Players drop into the space vacated by the previous passer. A sideways pass is followed by a forward run, a forward pass is followed by a sideways run. (If the ball is moving clockwise, the players are moving counter-clockwise.)

Different positions and strategies might require different movements (not all game situations will require aggressive forward movements after passing).

Kriss-Kross 9

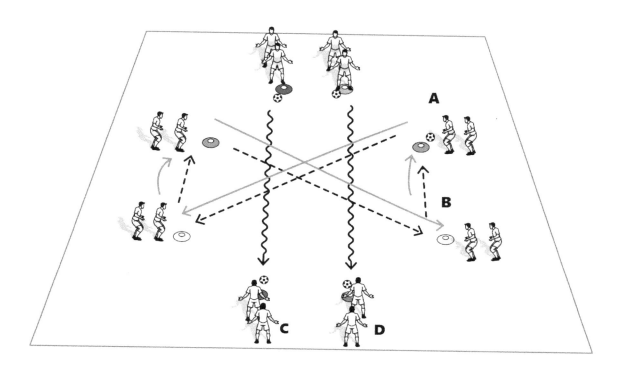

Rotation 4

Lines A and B pass and follow, while lines C and dribble across.

Diagonal pass and movement.

Progression

The player making the diagonal run plays a one-two with the player receiving, who then passes the ball off to the side.

Kriss-Kross 10

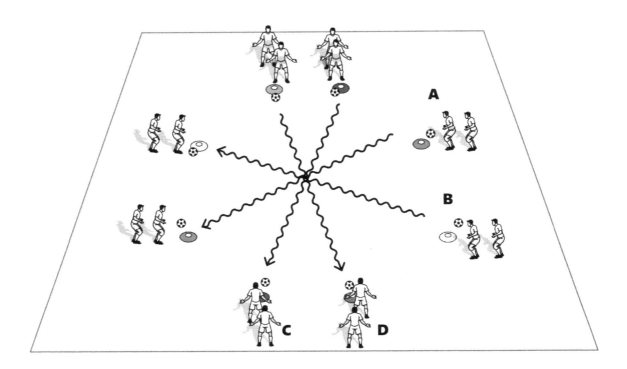

Central Point

Increased chaos for the dribblers with a specific spot where they all meet IF they all dribble in a straight line.

Players do not have to dribble in a straight line. Can they recognise the space and how to use it?

Kriss-Kross 11

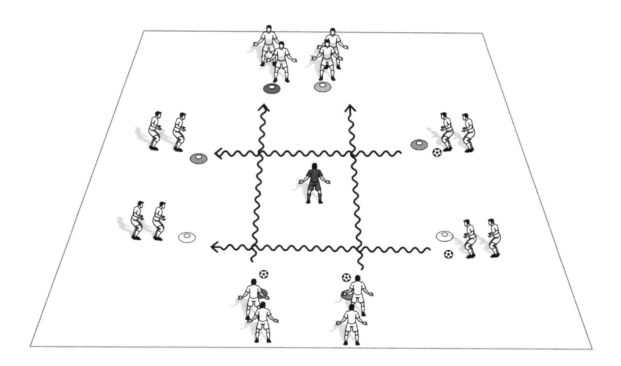

Defender

Dribble across the areas while avoiding the defender as well as the other dribblers

1. Defender has a bib in their hand, which they throw at the ball; if they hit the ball, swap with the player whose ball they hit.
2. Defender tries to win the ball with a tackle
3. Add another defender
4. Add more footballs to have eight dribblers

Kriss-Kross 12

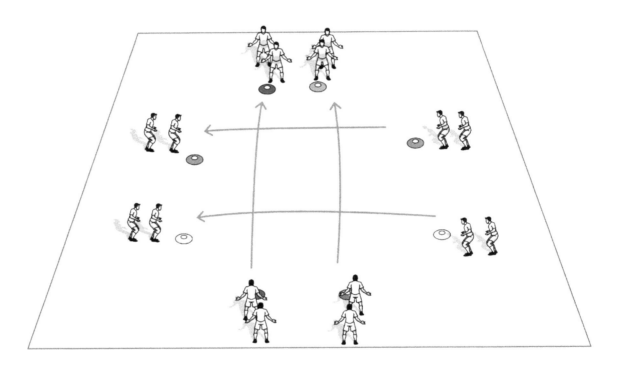

Physical

1. Players jog across from one side to the other, dodging others as they cross
2. Players sidestep
3. Players skip
4. Players use high knees/heel flicks
5. Players open/close the gates

The following are examples of how we might arrange the practices for different participant numbers.

Six Player Kriss-Kross

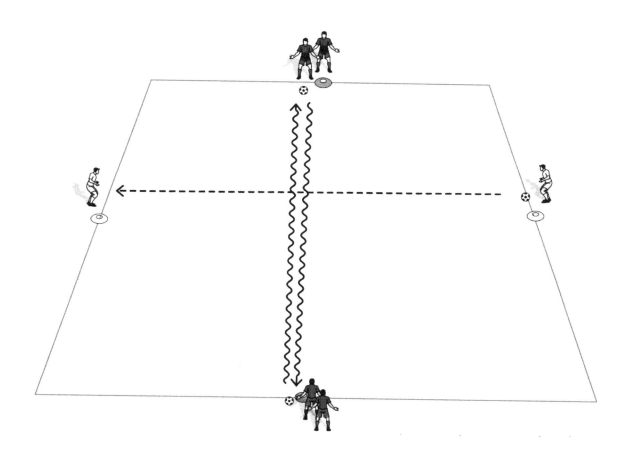

Nine Player Kriss-Kross

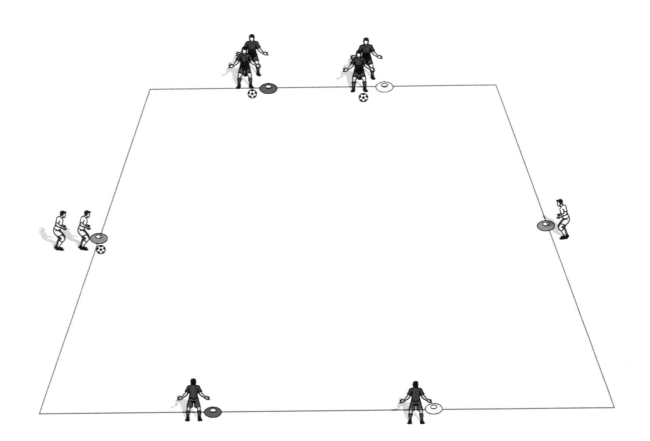

The Diamond

The diamond warm-up allows for dribbling and passing opportunities but has more emphasis on movement, before receiving, than the Kriss-Kross. In general, the easiest way to encourage players to move before receiving is by providing opposition that they need to move away from. There are opportunities to encourage these movements within our warm-up, but they may prove less effective than having to move away from the opposition. If our session design connects the warm-up and main portion of the practice, the relevant opposition should occur at that time. It is surprisingly common to see warm-up exercises that have little to no relevance to the main aim of the session; by including core elements of the game, the chances of a connecting thread should be increased.

Diamond 1

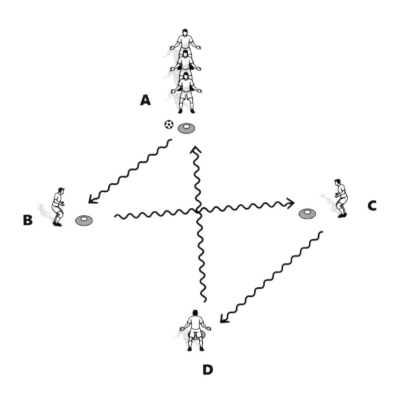

The ball starts at position A. A dribbles to B, B dribbles to C, C dribbles to D, D dribbles back to A. Can the players execute tricks as they dribble?

Progression 1

Change the direction. A to C, C to D, etc.

Progression 2

Add two more footballs to position A. The players at position A start to dribble when the player in front of them reaches position B.

Progression 3

The player at position D passes the ball back to position A.

Progression 4

The players perform a pre-determined number of movements before they begin their dribble. Ten toe taps, for example.

Diamond 2

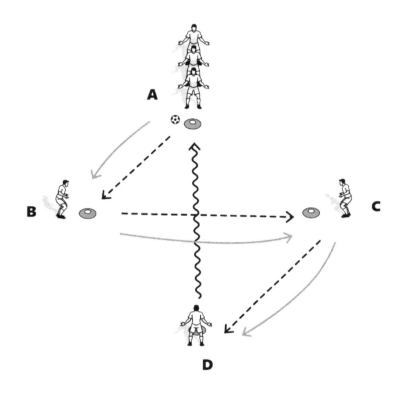

The ball starts at position A. From position A, the ball is passed to position B. Position B passes to position C. Position C passes to position D. Position D dribbles the ball back to position A. All players follow their passes.

Progression

The players MUST make a movement away from their cone before they receive. If possible, they should make a double movement away from the cone before receiving.

Diamond 3

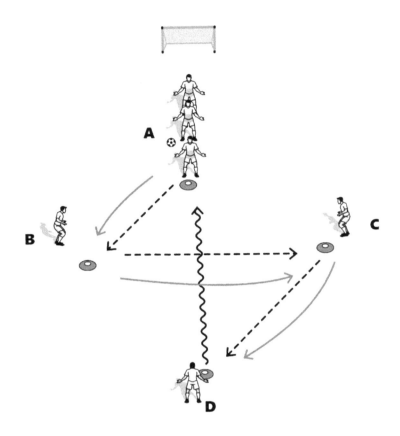

The ball starts at position A. From Position A, the ball is passed to position B, and then passed to position C. Position C passes to position D. Position D dribbles the ball back to position A and dribbles past the player at position A before finishing in the empty goal.

Progression

After shooting, the player goes in goal. After going in goal, the player joins the line for position A.

Real World

The Kriss-Kross session design is my go-to session for trials and new groups. It works for different ages and abilities, giving me an opportunity to observe the players and their abilities. The set up can easily be developed, changing the difficulty levels as required.

The task itself is simple, to get to the other side. The issue that players have is the chaos going on around them. Can they stay calm and remain focused? A combination of awareness and clarity will yield success, just as it will in a match. In some ways, the practice can be even more chaotic than a match. My message to the players is this. "If this is harder than a match, then when you play a match it should be no problem."

3
The Hexagon

"I am an admirer of dribbling. Two dribbles together change the content of a game; they clear things up, supply fresh oxygen, make the match more healthy."
Marcelo Bielsa

Dribblers are special. At one time, they were a dying breed in the game. Thankfully, that has changed, and we are seeing the return of players who are able to produce magic on the ball. We can thank the lawmakers who are offering greater protection to those who dribble; the often-crude challenges that would side-line players are being punished more harshly than they once were.

Dribbling is one of the most exciting strands of football. The sight of Jadon Sancho skipping around defenders consistently gets people out of their seats. We might consider there to be different types of dribblers: the player who relies on being fleet of foot to put their opponent off balance before accelerating away, or the player that uses body movement to shift the defender. Then we have the trickster – Neymar-like – using elaborate tricks to beat defenders (some might say humiliate defenders). All such players elicit reactions from crowds, team-mates, and opponents.

The reaction of opponents is of great interest. The idea of 'humiliation' is important as it makes defenders wary of getting too close to the dribbler, creating more time and space for that player on the ball. Not all 1v1 situations are equal. The player who can dominate a 1v1, either defensively or offensively, is at a great advantage. The dominant *defender* is not concerned by the opponent, not fearful of humiliation, and confident in their own ability to regain possession. The dominant *1v1 dribbler* is not fearful of the defender. They have no concerns that the presence of an opposing player will lead to the loss of possession.

It is my assertion that the key to effective dribbling is mentality. If a player has been constantly encouraged to pass the ball when faced with an opponent, that is likely to be their response when confronted by a defender in a match. However, if they have been encouraged to take on opponents, that is likely to be their response. The more they are exposed to 1v1 dribbling situations, the more likely they are to have success; they will gain confidence and competence, becoming more willing to dribble in game situations. Through 1v1 practices, players can gather the preparation they need and take that into our 3v3 situations, where the players will experience 1v1 but also 1v2 and 1v3. Should dribblers become competent in situations where they are outnumbered, we really will have game changers and potential match winners.

Imagine, for one moment, the Diego Maradona goal against England at the 1986 World Cup (no, not that one; the other one. The far greater, but less *infamous* of his two World Cup quarter-final goals). Maradona utilised his legendary low centre of gravity to spin, slalom, and trick his way past the England defence. To Maradona, the sight of an entire team in front of him was not enough to dissuade the mercurial number 10 from taking them on.

Likewise, in 1984, John Barnes scored a goal of legendary status against Brazil at the Maracana, coming in from the left side of the pitch, before holding off and going beyond several defenders and the goalkeeper, then scoring.

Lastly, the Brazilian Ronaldo – playing for Barcelona – captured the imagination of the world by dribbling at high speed past the Compostela defence in 1996. Starting in his own half, and using a combination of strength, speed, balance and exceptionally fast footwork, he scored a stunning goal. Football history is gilded with brilliant players scoring brilliant goals.

"Football is about joy. It's about dribbling. I favour every idea that makes the game beautiful." **Ronaldinho**

Exceptional dribblers can do other things to fearful teams. As alluded to, previously, dribblers often attract extra defenders. Teams will want to avoid the chaos created by an attacker slaloming their way through defensive lines, and the extra defenders concentrated on the dribbler will create space elsewhere. If our player has high levels of awareness and decision making, they will be able to exploit this. Indeed, a combination of 1v1s and other practices will help players to develop this skill.

Many of the great possession footballers have had fantastic ball manipulation skills. In recent times, Pirlo and Xavi are two of the greatest passers that football has seen. Yet both possessed the dribbling skills to retain possession in tight situations, eliminating opponents if they got too close too soon. Not all 1v1 situations are face to face, the defender may be approaching from the side or from behind, and players will need to have a picture of how to handle such scenarios. It was once said of Xavi that he never lost the ball because, by the time the opponent was there, the ball had gone. Because of Xavi's dribbling skills, he was also able to initiate pressure in order to pass *around* opponents, even though it was less apparent than the skillset of Neymar and co.

In a similar vein to the warming-up chapter, the set up here is designed to generate a high number of different practice options without having to change the practice layout too much. 'Repetition without repetition' is an oft-used term in relation to coaching. There are advantages to utilising the same set up as, once players have learned how it works, adjustments are easily picked up.

If a single set up is flexible enough to include 1v1s that occur face to face, from the side, and from behind – as well as connecting dribbling, possession, and finishing – then the practice will be of value to coaches at all levels.

The choice of shape is key to creating different angles and different options. As per below, players are maintained around the outside while still enabling players to face off in the centre. The Hexagon best fits a six-player design, while an Octagon might be used for eight players. For an odd number, two players may share a space.

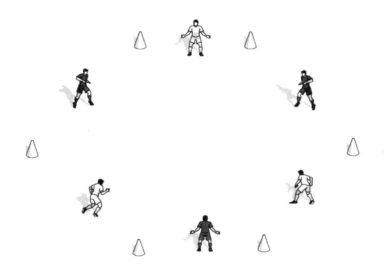

Moves

As one might imagine, the number of dribbling moves possible is huge, possibly even unquantifiable. Every move that a player sees can be adapted, then adapted again. From one move, we immediately have two new moves. Below is a list of moves that may be of use to players.

Sole taps   INSIDE TAPS   Brazilian toe taps   Outside taps

OUTSIDE, OUTSIDE, INSIDE   Inside, inside, outside   **Foot roll**

Outside roll, inside tap   Inside roll, outside tap

Pull push, inside   Pull push, outside   DRAG LACES

Drag chip/scoop   **Drag back**   Double drag   **Chop**

Double chop   Step over   Double step over

Step over turn   STEP KICK

Rivelinho step over (take the ball forward with the same foot that steps over the ball)

SHIMMY/SNAKE HIPS   Slap stepover (drag through legs into step over)

Heel toe   Wave   **Cruyff**

Reverse Cruyff/Joe Cole   Hocus Pocus   VEE OUTSIDE

VEE INSIDE   **Triangles, inside**   Triangles, outside

TRIANGLES, SOLE   **McGEADY SPIN**   **Zidane**

Maradona   Roulette   Berbatov spin

La croquetta (Iniesta move)   U-Turn   INSIDE TWIST OFF

OUTSIDE TWIST OFF   **Side step**   **Double side step**   Rabona

Rainbow flick   Lambretta (Djalminha's rainbow flick)

Flick-Flack   Elastico   Matthews move

Ball stand   Inside cut   **Outside cut**   Sombrero

Fake shot into drag back/chop/vee/hocus pocus etc etc etc

Hexagon 1

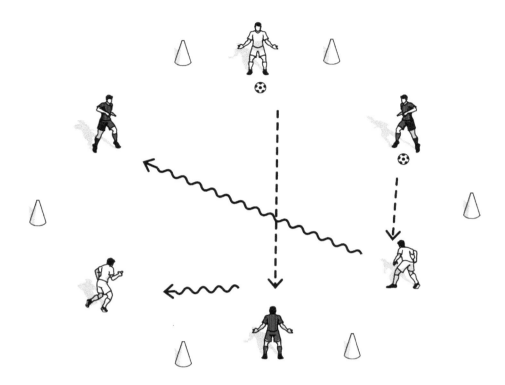

Play starts with the player with the ball passing across into the opposition player (stripe to white, white to stripe). The receiving player attempts to take on the opposition player to the right of the passer (their left) and dribble out of the octagon. If the defender wins the ball, they try to dribble out of the octagon through the gate of the opponent.

Progression 1

The player receiving can dribble out of any gate belonging to an opponent. The defenders can move to cover any gate and are not stuck at their initial gate.

Progression 2

The receiving player can escape through any gate (except their own). Defenders need to move to cover the escape routes.

Points

- Awareness
- Change of direction
- Acceleration
- Tricks/skills

Hexagon 2

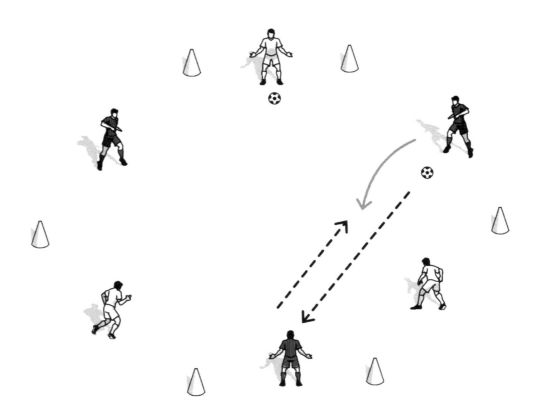

Pass, set, and dribble. The player in possession can attack any of the white team's defenders and their gate.

Progression 1

The passer and the setter join together to attack any of the white team defenders and their gate.

Start with only one ball in play (whether it is the 1v1 or 2v2). Later, have two balls in play to increase the traffic and awareness required for success.

Hexagon 3

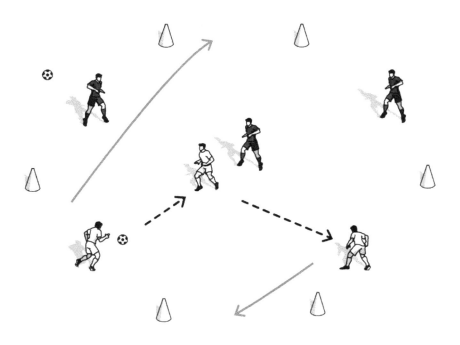

1v1 Possession

The players in the middle may only use their teammates to retain possession. If a stripe wins the ball, they use the outside players to retain the ball. The outside players may need to move to empty spaces to better support the player in possession. Players in the middle play for one minute before switching.

Progression 1

If the team with the ball makes three passes, the central player can dribble out of either of the vacant gates to score a point. The next two players come in. After four rounds, which team has the most points?

Progression 2 – Rotation.

The player who passes into the middle follows their pass and takes up a position in the middle. After passing to the outside, the central player follows their pass.

Points

- Movement
- Support
- Angles
- Distances
- Quality of pass

Hexagon 4

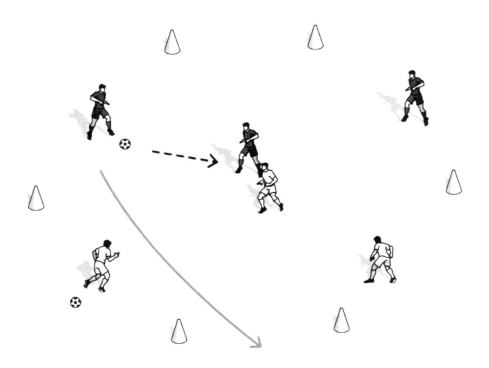

1v1 Possession 2

Outside players hold the ball in their hands, except for the player with a ball at his feet. The striped players look to keep possession, whilst the white team tries to win the ball and then go out of the area by dribbling past any of the stripes. Should the white team succeed in dribbling the ball out, they will receive another ball from a white teammate (who drops the ball they are holding to their feet) at the restart, and stripes will look to regain possession and dribble out past a white.

The 'ball in the hands' approach enables a quick restart after the ball has gone out. Players for the team in possession may need to move to the empty space to better support their teammate(s).

Points

- Communication
- Movement
- Quality of pass

Hexagon 5

Finishing

The player in possession (the stripe) can score in any of the goals protected by the opposition (if you do not have actual goals, use cones). The player protecting the goals may use their hands as a goalkeeper. If the goalkeeper saves, and the ball stays in play, whoever gets it has control of the game. If the goalkeeper keeps hold of the ball, they play to a teammate. White scores against stripe, stripe scores against white. Should a player score, they collect a ball from one of their teammates on the outside. If they shoot and miss, the opposition gets a ball and attacks. When all the balls have been used, swap the players in the middle.

Progression

The inside player can pass to any of their team-mates around the outside to score.

Points

- Movement
- Change of direction
- Types of finish (the further the goals are back from the gate, the more likely it is that the chip or scoop will be used)

Hexagon 6

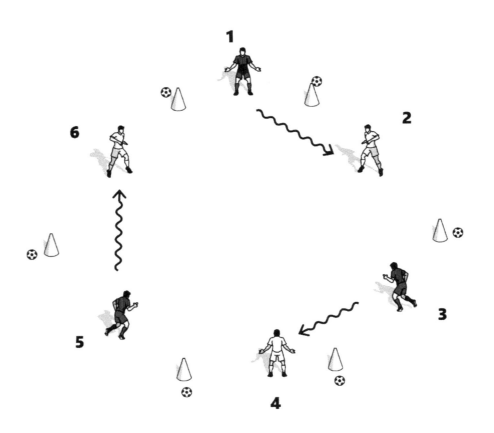

- 1v1 | 1v2| 3v4 | 5v6

The player with the ball looks to dribble through their opponents' gates.

Progress and change the angles of approach by stacking the opposition.

- 1v3 | 2v6 | 4v5

Change again.

- 1v6 | 2v4 | 3v5

Continue to change as desired.

Points

- Angles of approach
- Body shape
- Acceleration
- Tricks/skills

Hexagon 7

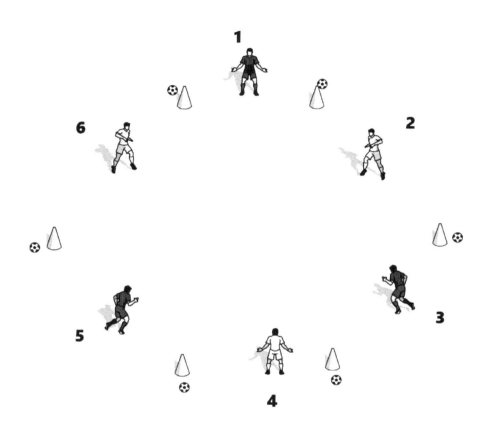

1v1v1 x2

Two multiplayer games take place at the same time, 1v3v5 and 2v4v6. Players score by dribbling through the gates of the opposition.

Progression

Add in goals behind the gates for players to score in.

Points

- Pressure on the ball
- Protect the ball
- Manipulate the ball
- Accelerate
- Change of direction

Hexagon 8

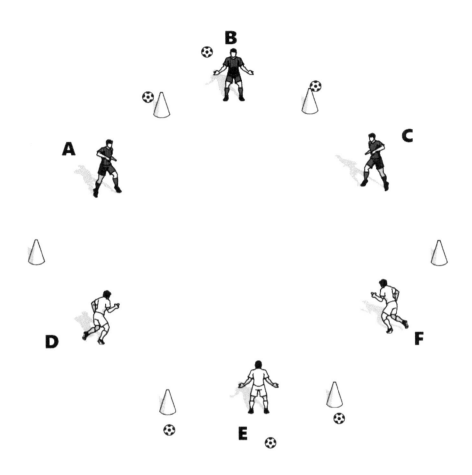

3v3

The stripes protect the gates marked A, B, and C. The whites protect the gates marked D, E, and F. The team in possession scores by dribbling out of the opposition gates.

Progression

Play 2v2 with two supporting players.

Points

- Movement
- Orientated touch
- Protect the ball
- Tricks and Fakes
- Changes of speed and direction

Real World

The hexagon developed from the octagon, originally an eight-sided practice inspired by mixed martial arts. Players were trapped inside, competing one on one. However, an octagon was confusing in a 3v3 context so was developed into a hexagon. The environment created by the hexagon can be a highly competitive and testing for 'one versus...' situations, with players deploying their skills in order to succeed.

When looking at practice design, I try to consider efficiency. Can we use the same layout for differing outcomes? In one versus one practice, it is important to consider that not all one versus one situations are face-to-face. The hexagon creates angles and a variety of receiving situations without making drastic changes to the setup, allowing players to encounter more scenarios that are relevant to their matchday experiences.

4
Variables

Everything can be changed.

Whether that is a mindset, or a setup, nothing is fixed. The only thing that prevents change is whether we really want to change or not.

Usually, we apply grand overarching thoughts such as the above to equally grand moments in life, but the idea of how much we want to change affects smaller areas too. Even how a football pitch looks.

In our minds, we all have an image of what a football pitch looks like. The goals, the lines, the number of players. We know what a game of football looks like. If we distil that down, how much can we get rid of, and still have a game of football?

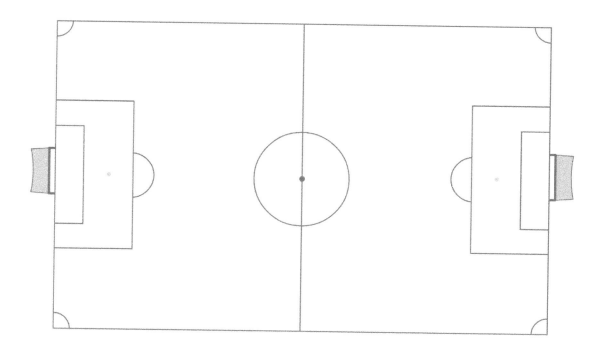

We can begin by removing the corner quadrants and the D on the edge of the penalty boxes. The remaining area is certainly still recognisable as a football pitch.

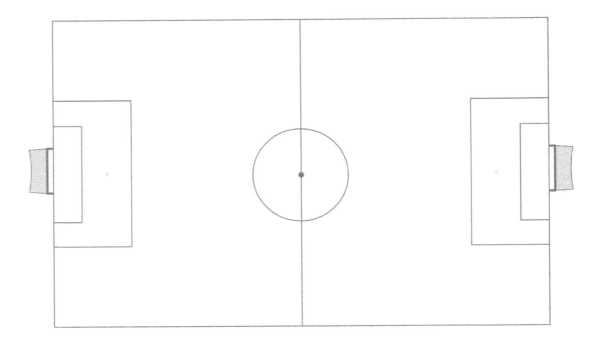

If we then remove the centre circle that should have little effect on the way we play the game. Removing the penalty spots might be a slight inconvenience, but players should be able to work around that easily. The playing area still looks like a football pitch and would operate like one.

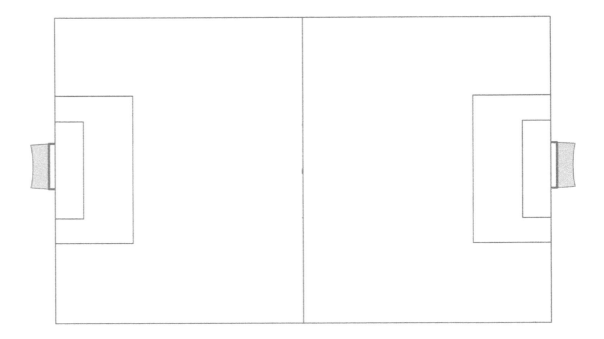

Removing the six-yard box would change very little. Especially if we consider that there are varying regulations in junior football around where the goalkeeper can place the ball when restarting. Removing the halfway line may cause a few issues with regard to restarts and offside, but beyond these moments, the game would remain largely the same. The layout is still recognisable as a football pitch.

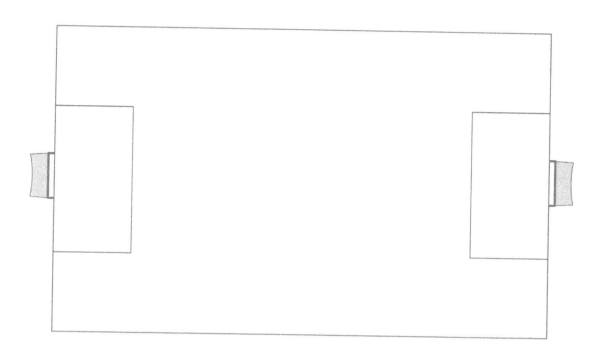

There are only three remaining options to remove. The penalty areas, the goals, and the external markings.

Chapter 4

Removing the penalty areas leaves an area that is still recognisably useable for football. Arguably, we could leave the goals and remove the external lines and still play a game. The removal of the lines slowly erodes the rules of the game, but a game is still possible.

Changing the layout challenges our perception of what the game is, but also, by moving the lines, we can explore what is possible, taking away some restrictions to tasks. Conversely, we can add more lines and areas to change the pitch and the space available. Different spaces create different challenges. This environmental approach creates implicit learning for players, giving them space to breathe and play, while also leaving opportunities for the coach to step in as and when required.

Leaving the lines but removing the goals gives us a useable area but takes away the objective of the game. We may then surmise that, in order to have a game of football, we must have goals. Goals give the game direction. It is possible for us to remove goals from the setup and, in doing so, the emphasis would then shift to other elements such as passing, dribbling, awareness, and use of space. However, players are unlikely to accept a game without goals as a game. We can change the goals to change the challenge, though. Bigger goals, smaller goals, multiple goals, all of these changes will provide different tasks and outcomes. Using two mini goals at one end will affect the way that players use space, as the natural action of defenders is to align themselves with the goal. In a game with multiple goals, the players will not be able to effectively align themselves with all goals. They must, therefore, prioritise – which will affect both the defending team and the attacking team, changing the balance between tight spaces and open spaces.

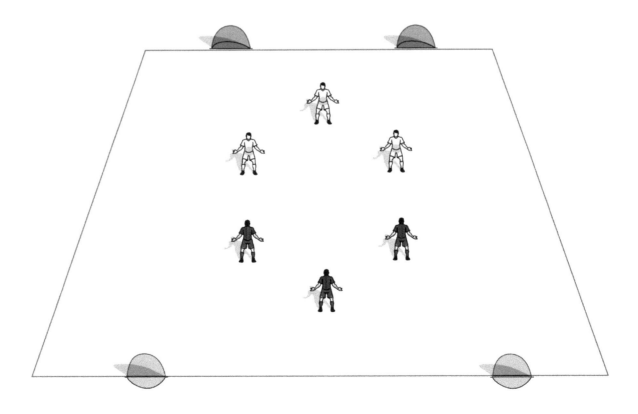

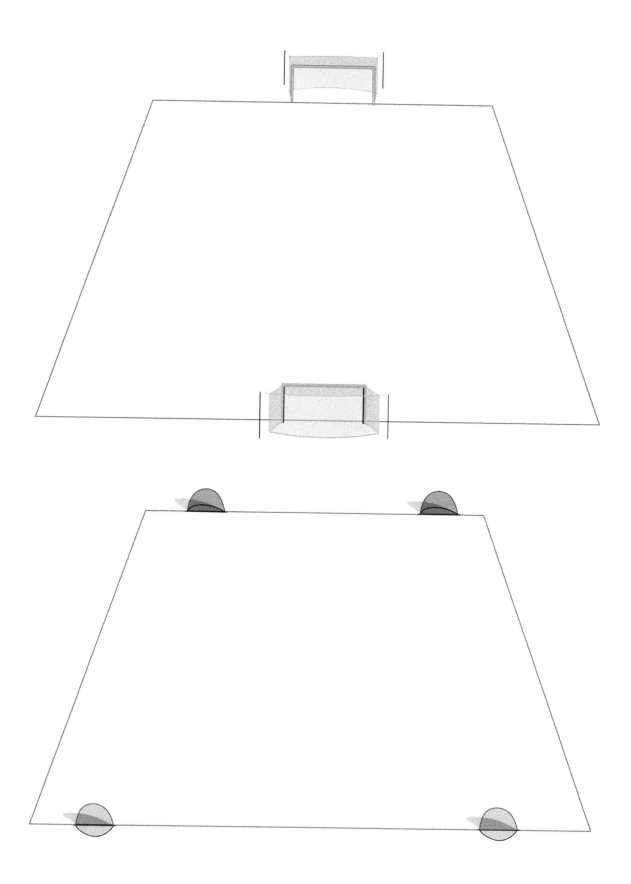

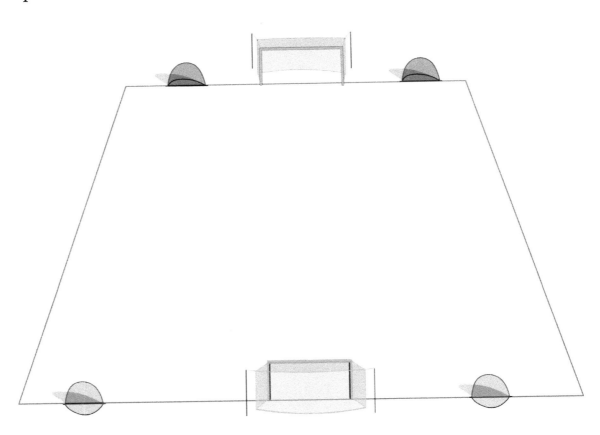

We can place different values on the different goals. If the side goals are worth fewer points than the large goal, teams and players then have a decision to make about where they attack and where they defend. What do they prioritise, and what are they prepared to give up?

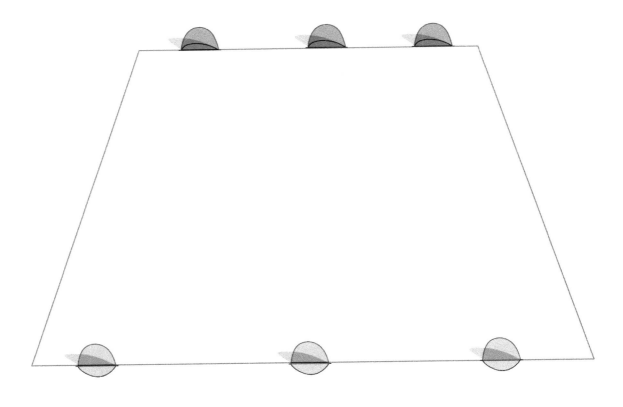

Taking the same principles to extremes, by moving the goals around the pitch, the directional nature of the game can become fluid. A 360-degree game can be created that retains a goalscoring objective. Such setups can also enable multi-team games.

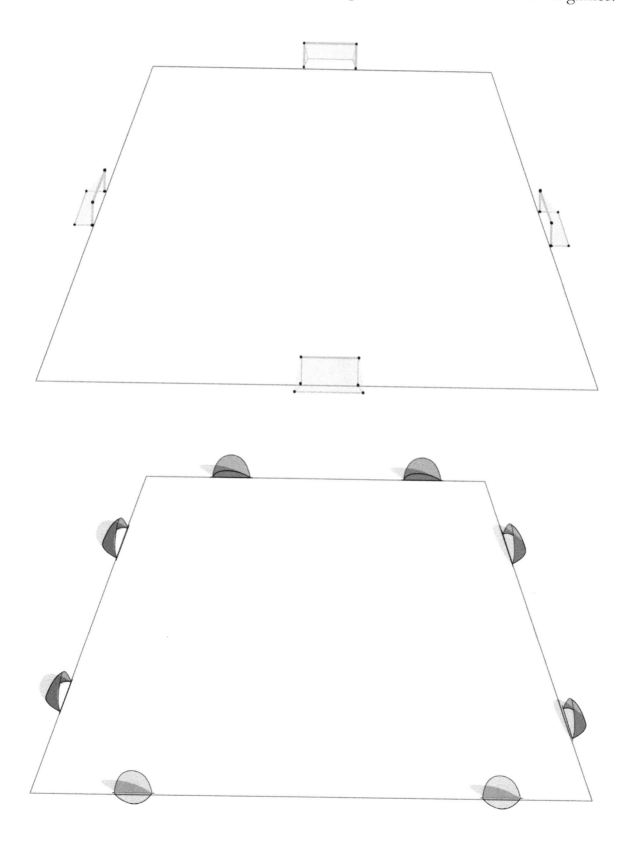

Chapter 4

When identifying the characteristics of a game of football, most people would identify two teams facing off against each other. This does not mean that we cannot change this variable. The question is, why would we do so? The aim here would be to increase interference and levels of chaos/difficulty for the players. Chaos enforces greater awareness upon players, but chaos can also equate to fun, challenge, and engagement.

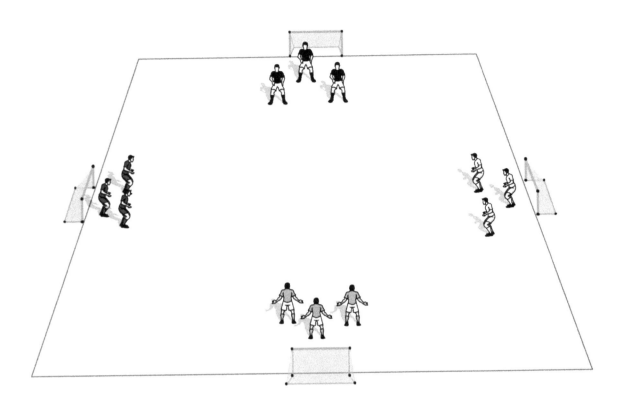

In the example above, two footballs would be in play. One for the teams playing horizontally, and one for the teams playing vertically. The ball is another key variable to the game of football. We regularly use different sizes of football for different age groups, giving the younger age groups smaller footballs, and those aged fifteen and above the maximum size. The size of the ball changes the task at hand. A smaller football for an older player would be more difficult to dribble and strike, while a larger football for younger players can be more difficult to dribble due to the relative size of the ball to the player.

The size of the ball is not the only variable we have to work with. Changing the degree of inflation for a ball can affect the players' actions. Using a heavier or lighter ball, a ball with more or less grip, using a ball with less bounce, these are all options we can use to add variety to our training sessions.

A further option is to change the ball completely. Using a tennis ball pushes the idea of the increased difficulty of a decreased ball size. Changing to a ball from a different sport can alter the anticipation skills required and the touch required to bring the ball under control. Rugby balls and mini American footballs are particularly challenging. The important factor is not that a football is being used, but that a ball is being kicked, or possibly more precisely, *not being handled.*

Having changed the area, the goals, and the ball, there remains one final aspect of the game to change. The number of participants. The entire premise of the 3v3 idea is built around changing the number of players involved in order to increase the opportunities for individuals. Within the construct of 3v3, the balance can be altered depending on how we wish to challenge our players. Even teams do not necessarily equate to fair teams. Equal teams may not represent a realistic challenge.

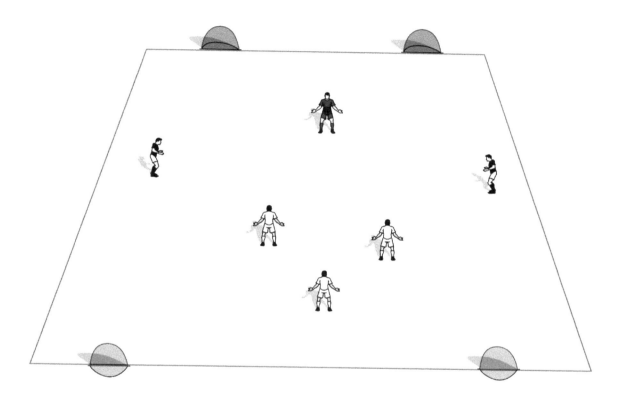

This scenario is 3v1 with two neutral players. This would be heavily overloaded in favour of the white team when in possession. They would effectively have a 5v1 – a huge advantage. This is an extreme example of how the balance can be changed (which may be of use if we have a number of players really struggling).

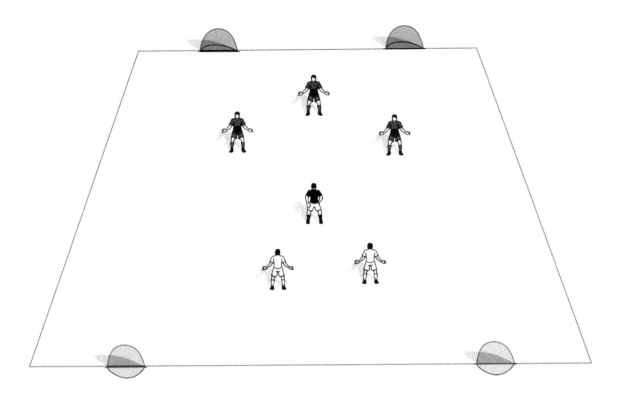

This situation utilises 3v2+1. Far less extreme than a 5v1 in possession, the stripes will have a 4v2 and the whites 3v3. Having a two-player advantage is a greater advantage than just a one-player advantage; we would reasonably expect to enable the stripes to create more goalscoring opportunities than the whites, yet the white team would be able to have some success when defending.

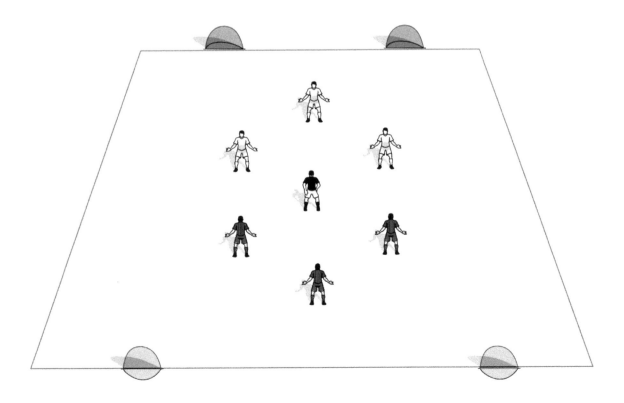

The 3v3 +1 creates an advantage for whichever team is in possession; however, a single-player advantage should not be so great that defensive success is impossible (depending on the ability of the players).

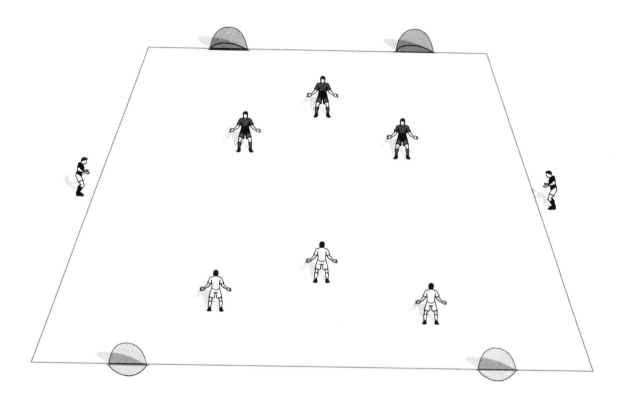

A 3v3 +2 creates a two-player overload. These extra players may operate within the playing area, or operate on the outside (the end lines by the goal are also an option).

The 3v3 +1 and 3v3 +2 options are also an alternative for coaches who have a 3v3 plan, but their numbers at training fluctuate.

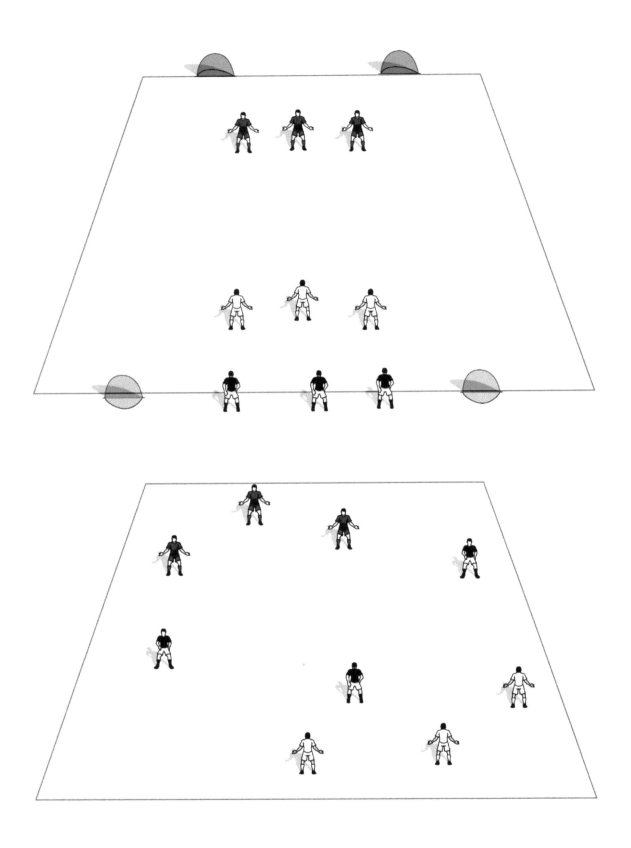

For nine players, 3v3+3 or 3v3v3 are options. The principles of transition can come to the fore in such exercises, with teams playing in waves and looking to regroup or regain after losing the ball.

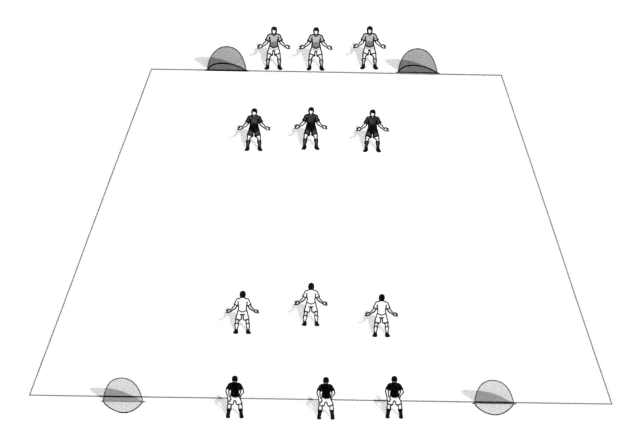

3v3v3v3 is an extension of the above, incorporating more players but also increasing the options for the transition.

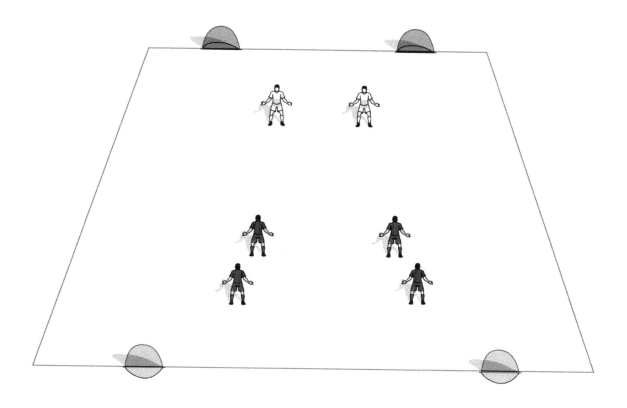

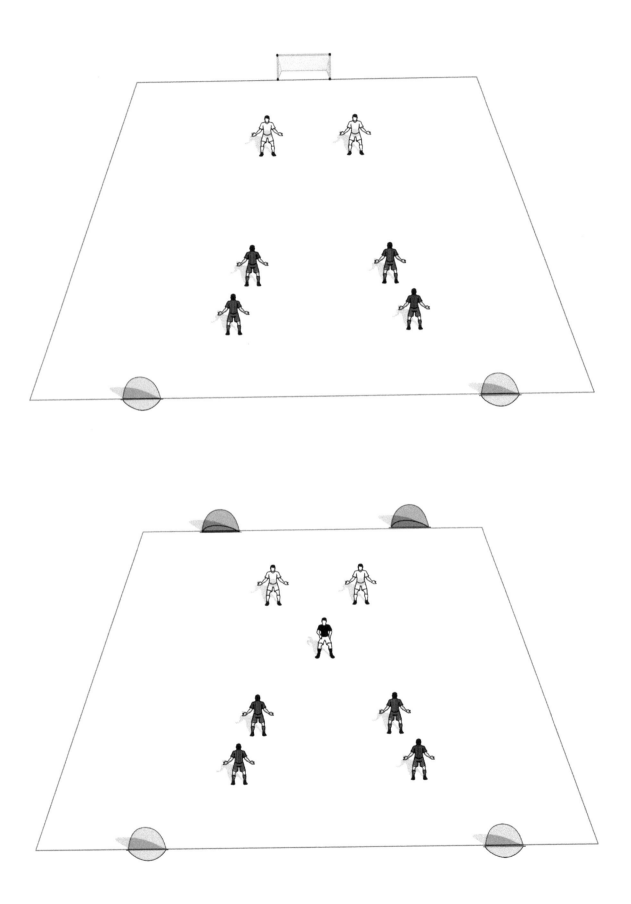

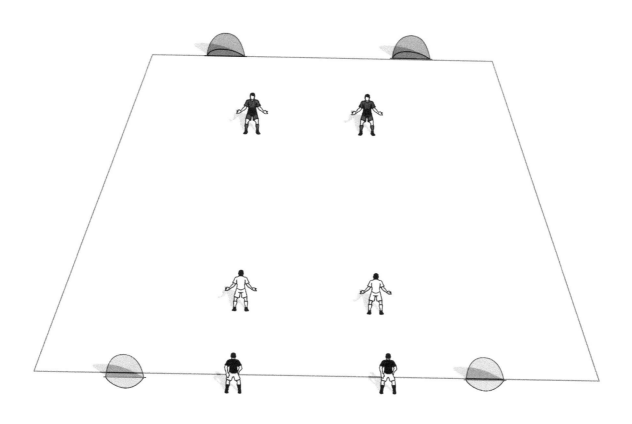

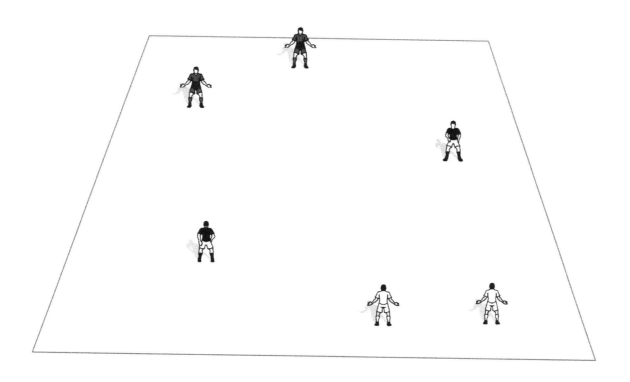

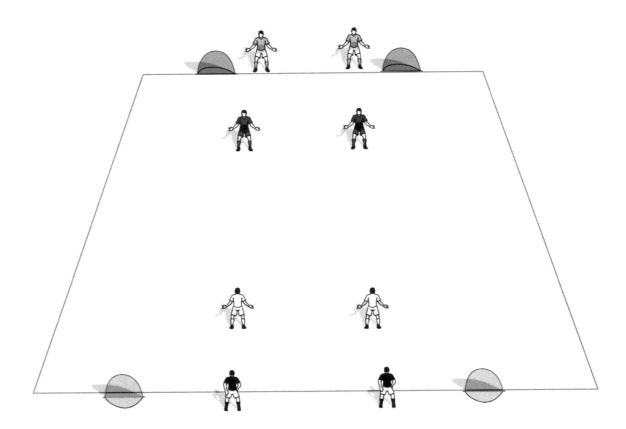

Without using any complex rules or conditions, coaches can create environmental challenges for players and opportunities for coaches to help players when they arise. By using the environment, players have opportunities to breathe and solve problems on their own before turning to the coach, while the coach can cast their expert eye before attending to anything they observe. Plus, the players get to do what they like the most, *play the game*. Or at least a version of it!

Real World

As coaches, we are often looking for equal numbers during match times at our sessions. Often, we solve the problem of having nine players by using a magic man, but there are other solutions available that present players with alternative scenarios.

If one of the nine players is a goalkeeper, this provides us with opportunities to link sessions to building from the back, forwards pressing, or other final-third related practices.

Few coaches of grassroots clubs will be fortunate enough to have more than one specialist goalkeeper. At younger age groups, this is no problem (and there is a very strong argument for not having a specialist goalkeeper until much later. In one under 8s team I coached, we had no specialist goalkeeper but four excellent goalkeepers). With older groups, I have faced this situation many times. The personnel have driven the practice design.

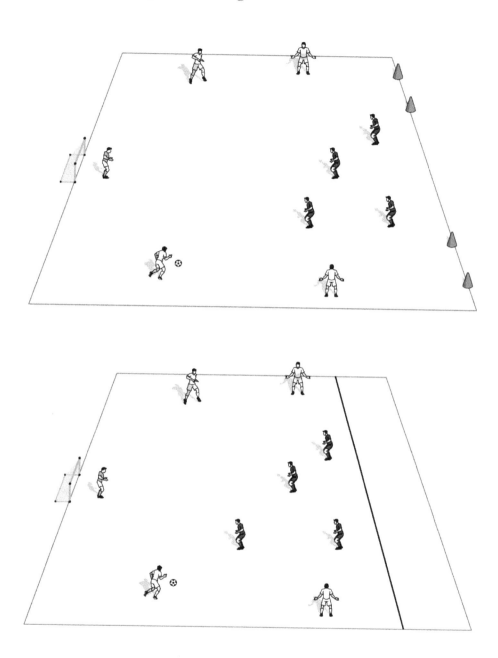

The two teams will have different but relevant objectives. In both images, the stripes will be aiming to score a goal. In image one, the white team is trying to score in either of the gates. If you had mini goals, this would work even better. In image two, the white team is aiming to run the ball into the end zone or pass the ball to a teammate in the end zone.

Both types of practice have been used to encourage defenders to be more positive when in possession, and to try to turn defence into attack.

5
Goal Creation

The ability to create goals is a vital part of the modern footballer's arsenal. Creation is not just in the realm of forward players either. More fluid formations and patterns mean that assists could come from almost any position. While it is typically the goal scorers who are lauded as heroes, they often owe a great deal to their suppliers. Rare is the player who is capable of scoring the magic 20 goals a season without the assistance of teammates. As much as we might dream of the player who scores glorious solo goals – game upon game – only a handful of players in history have been capable of this. We need to create.

The great creators are great decision-makers, comprehending where and when to play just the right pass at just the right time, sometimes using a dribble to entice opponents in and creating the space for their teammates to strike.

Dennis Bergkamp was famed as an assist master. His great skill was in finding a way through an opposition defence, when no way through seemed possible. Pivoting in tight central areas to thread passes through to forwards who were only too grateful to accept their gifts.

While David Beckham's ability to whip free-kicks over the wall into the top corner undoubtedly helped to create his legend, his ability to pick out a teammate in the penalty area from wide positions also played a big role. Beckham possessed the capability to deliver from almost any position on the right side of the pitch, curving deliveries with the inside of his foot, away from the goalkeeper and towards oncoming strikers.

When Beckham joined Real Madrid, he joined another assist king, Guti. Guti's gift was to make the goalscoring as easy as possible for teammates, often turning down chances of his own in the knowledge that the chance for his teammate would be even better.

Under Pep Guardiola, Manchester City has sought to make goalscoring as simple as possible by removing the goalkeeper from the equation, picking out players at the far post to sweep the ball into the biggest possible space.

These players and teams are not the only ones who have had the ability to unlock teams; football history is littered with them. Guardiola's teams are significant because they have a plan around how they will score goals. The objective is to work the ball into areas that increase their chances to score. Guardiola's teams are built around possession football but most goals are scored in roughly the same way, no matter the style of play. With a one- or two-touch finish within the penalty area, in a zone the width of the six-yard box, and out to the penalty spot. A counter-attacking team will also work the ball into these positions; the difference may be in how the ball gets there.

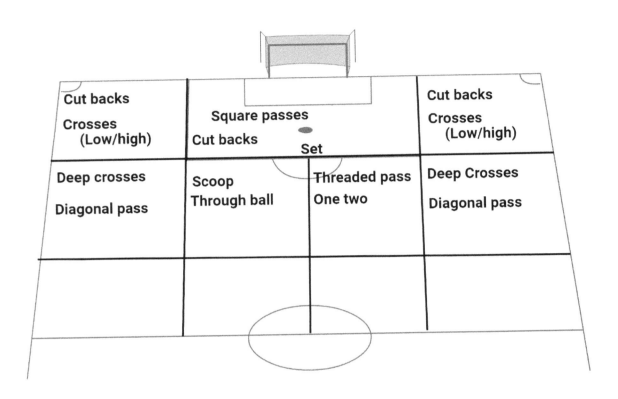

If we can identify where the assists come from, we can then identify how we get into those positions. The "second assist" or the pass before the assist. A deep cross may be followed by a cutback or square pass. A threaded pass may be followed by a low cross. The zones from which assists occur are where opponents will seek to protect but, in protecting one area, they will become weak in another. The trend, in recent times, has been to pack the centre of the pitch, blocking zone 14 and the half-spaces, making the wide positions increasingly important. As so many wide players now play on opposite or inverted sides, this has meant that attacking full-backs have become an increasing source of assists.

Passes, alone, are not enough either. Movement without the ball makes everything possible. The movement will link with the areas that goals or scored or created. As will movements with the ball.

Core movements

- One-twos
- Overlaps
- Underlaps

- Set and spins
- Cross overruns/switches of position
- Forward runs

Football may change again, returning to 'longer passes into space' as teams condense their play into one half, leaving space behind them. This tactic is often used by teams who expect their opponents to dominate possession against them. Leicester City, for example, will allow the opposition to dominate possession against them to allow Jamie Vardy the space to exploit his pace. Or even playing long into a static fixed forward, laying the ball off for forward runners. If the game does evolve in this way, then the way in which we practice chance creation will change accordingly.

"In most scenarios, it isn't the man on the ball who decides where the ball goes, but the players without the ball. Their running actions determine the next pass."
Johan Cruyff

Game 1

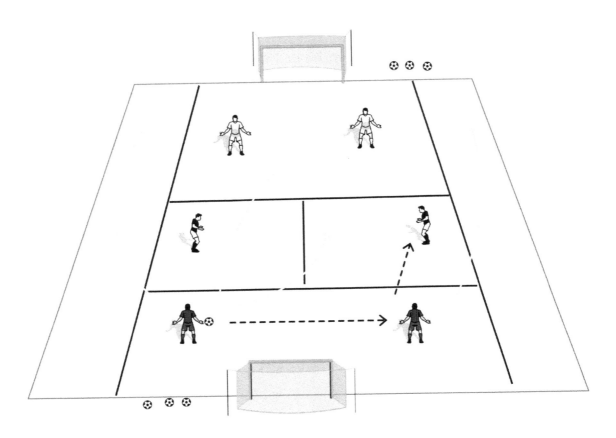

A 2v2 plus 2 practice. Goals can only be scored in the final third. Players can make forward runs into any area after passing into either of the black-shirted central players. The role of the black-shirted players is to look for an assist or "second assist".

The markings of the area are designed to replicate the parts of the pitch from which assists and second assists will occur.

Game 2

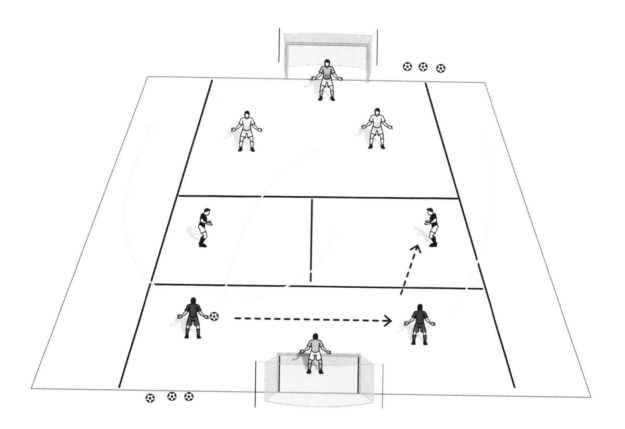

A 2v2 plus 2 practice with goalkeepers. Goals can only be scored in the final third. Players can make forward runs into any area passing into either of the black-shirted players. The role of the black-shirted players is to look for an assist or "second assist".

Progression

The black-shirted players can score, either from the central area or the final third.

Game 3

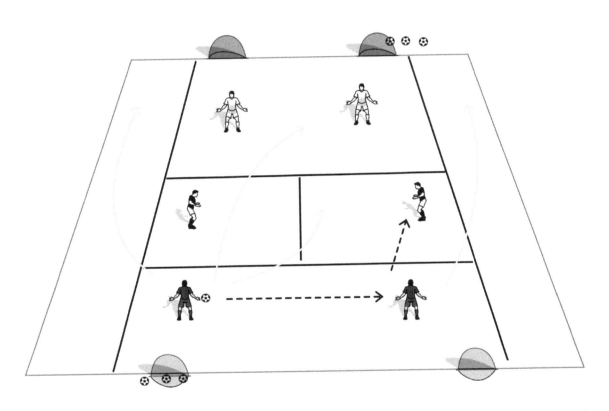

A 2v2 plus 2 practice. Goals can only be scored in the final third. Players can make forward runs into any area after passing into the black-shirted players. The role of the black-shirted players is to look for an assist or "second assist".

The use of two goals changes the positioning of defenders and the recognition of space.

Game 4

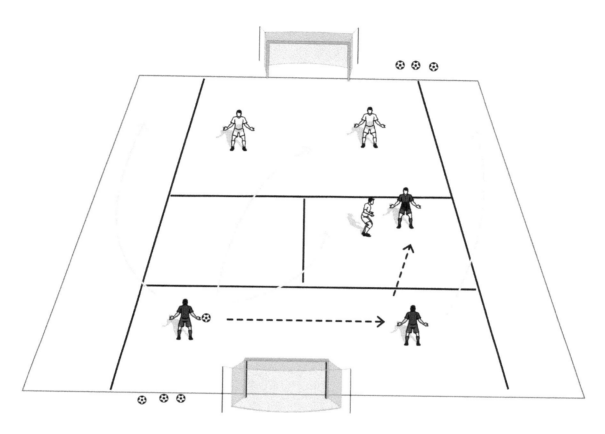

Players can make forward runs into any area after passing into the central player. There is a 1v1 battle in the middle.

Progression 1

Allow players to dribble into the middle zones to create a 2v1.

Progression 2

Add goalkeepers.

Attacking midfielders will often operate in positions where they are screened or marked by a defensive midfielder. They will have to work to find space in the zone, or teammates will need to move into the zone in order to outnumber the defensive midfielder. The solution, defensively, is to use a second defensive midfielder.

Game 5

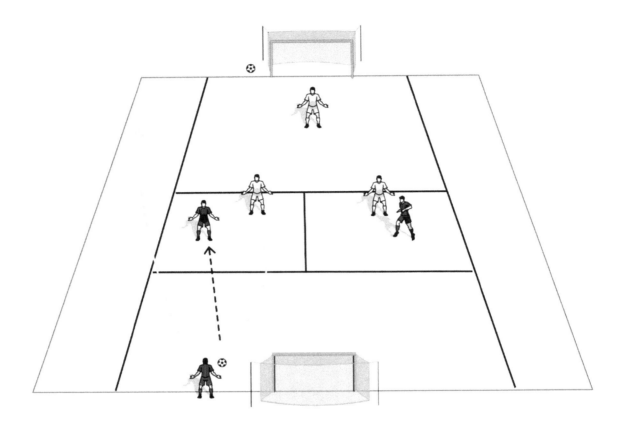

Play begins beside the goal. The striped-player looks to pass into either of the two stripes in the centre. The central players are locked into their square. After the pass, players can make runs into wide channels or the final third, trying to combine and score. If the whites win the ball, they can attack.

Progression 1

Allow the central player from the team in possession to drop into the defensive third to help play forward.

Progression 2

The player restarting the game can dribble into the centre.

Game 6

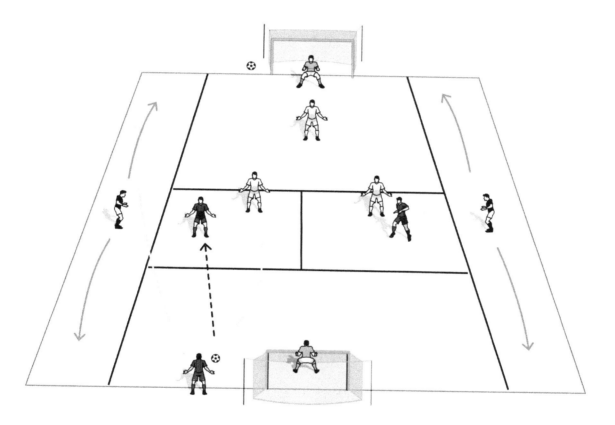

As with game 5 but with added goalkeepers and wide players. Positions are representative of key attacking positions and roles for chance creation.

How can the goalkeepers support the play in possession?

How does the presence of the wide players affect the forward runs?

Game 7

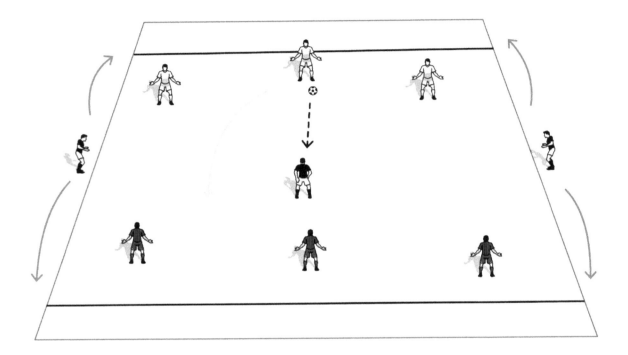

Teams score by playing into, or dribbling into, the opposition's end zone.

If the pass into the end zone comes from one of the black-shirted players, score three points.

Points

- Playmakers
- Overlaps
- Underlaps
- One-twos
- Forward runs

Relative to the other practices, this has more emphasis on movement off the ball, aiming to give the player in possession more options to pass to forward runners.

Game 8

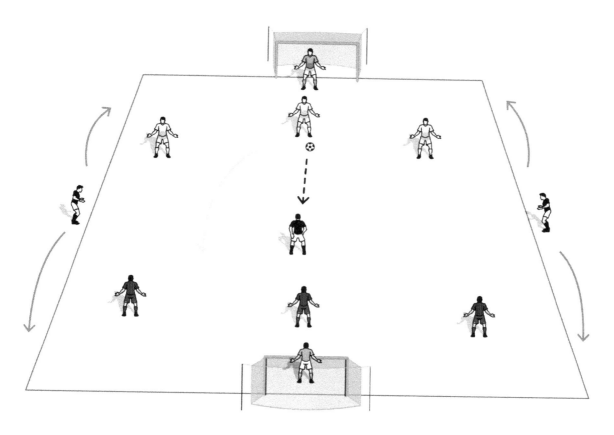

Teams play 3v3 plus two wide players, a central playmaker, and two goalkeepers.

One point for scoring.

Three points for scoring after an assist from a black-shirted team player.

Points

- Playmaking
- Overlaps
- Underlaps
- One-twos
- Forward passes

Chapter 5

Real World

Although my preference is to work with teams and players before they have entered into 11v11 football, I have worked with many sides playing 11v11. So often, their biggest problem is being unable to score (or unable to score enough). Teams produce good approach play and have lots of shots, but are unable to find the net. Then, they are puzzled as to why this is the case.

Most often, the reason behind a team's inability to find the net will be that they have no clear plan on how to score. They do not have a plan to exploit the key areas where goals are created; the areas often referred to as half-spaces or wide areas. As a result, they take shots from areas with low chances of scoring. Once teams have an understanding of the areas they need to work the ball into (to produce an assist or second assist), the quality behind chances becomes much better, and the goals start to flow. Making goalscoring less difficult leads to more goals, particularly if all the players have an understanding of the plan.

It is important to point out to the players that this plan is the ideal. This is not to say they cannot, or should not, score in another way; players must play what they see in front of them, but they may also need something to fall back on when they are unclear on what is in front of them.

With one team, the idea of playing the ball into a channel for a runner to cross low led to some highly adventurous play, with the full-back crossing low for the other full-back to apply the tap in. This happened because they understood the spaces to exploit, and *how* they should exploit them.

6
3v3 Finishing

Goal scoring can hide a number of flaws.

Recently, one of the youth teams I work with faced a team with a deadly striker. We played them twice during the same festival and both teams were well matched. Except that whenever this forward received the ball, he scored. Touch. Strike. Goal. Control with the left, finish with the right. Control with the right, finish with the left. The margin of victory was three goals but the gap between the sides in performance terms was far closer. Exceptional finishing made the difference.

Through the levels of professional and semi-professional football, you will find managers stating that the difference between the top and the bottom is the quality in both penalty areas. Or, as a number of players at the hyper-competitive National League level in England have said to me, you only as good as your strikers.

This is an era in which goalscoring has moved away from the typical penalty box poacher, the speed merchant who thrives on long passes behind defences, or the physically dominant header of the ball. There are players who possess these attributes. Aguero is a phenomenal penalty box poacher. Jamie Vardy, Timo Werner and Pierre Emerick Aubamayang all possess great pace and will race onto any passes behind defences. Harry Kane is excellent in the air. However, players cannot be reliant on one specific attribute and expect prolonged success (unless that attribute is the ability to waltz through defences and finish). This is an era of goalscoring wide players, or wide players converted into strikers. And forwards cutting inside from wide areas and arriving at far post positions. Goal scoring has changed. The same types of goal are scored, but with a different frequency to previous eras. Whether that is permanent change, who can say…

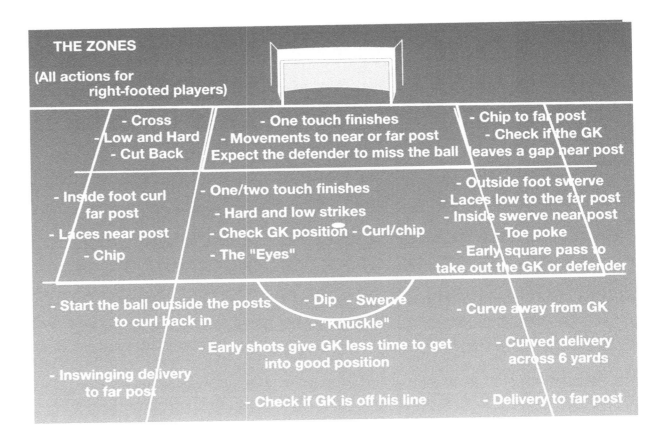

The true masters of the goalscoring art are capable of such a variety of finishes that it is an intimidatingly demanding task to stop them. Certain players are superb exponents of a particular type of finish to the degree that it has become synonymous with them. Thierry Henry had the curved finish into the bottom right-hand corner. Romario was the master of the toe poke finish. Francesco Totti's ability to chip goalkeepers was unparalleled. None of these players relied on this specific finish to score goals, but they bore their signatures.

A common conceit of pundits and columnists is that goalscorers are born, not made. Comments such as "instinctive" and "you can't coach that" are often thrown around when it comes to strikers. This may depend on how we define things. If we define coaching as explicit instruction, we may not be able to coach every player in that way. For some players, this may be precisely what they need to reach the next level of prowess, though. The most famous example being the work between Rene Meulensteen and Cristiano Ronaldo to progress a precocious winger into an efficient predator.

If we define coaching as the creation of opportunities to learn – whether the learning is through explicit direction or implicit designs – then goalscoring must be considered as coachable to all. Put simply, if players do not have opportunities to score goals, they will struggle to improve their goal scoring. What we must then look for is a 'goalscoring environment'.

In the first Developing Skill book, few practices were dedicated to goalscoring; either the creation of the chance or the finish itself. Instead, the majority of designs included goals as a way to conclude a passage of play and help provide direction to the practice. The act of scoring would be practised, but was not the primary focus for practice.

Developing Skill: Practices that focused on creating and finishing

- Diamond shooting
- Reversed goals
- Attacking waves
- Splitting passes
- Killer moment
- Waves + goalkeepers
- Forward runs
- Overloaded attacks
- Link with wide players

This chapter is dedicated to the creating and scoring of goals. The designs aim to give players high levels of repetition, which small groups should enable. There are opportunities for players to practise under no pressure, light pressure, medium pressure, high pressure and beyond, all depending on the stage that the players are at, and where it sits within the session. The objective is also to avoid complicated passing patterns and movements leading up to the shot. There are some passing patterns involved, but the aim is for them to be simple. Most importantly, players are not waiting a significant length of time for their next shooting opportunity.

The practices are also designed with the assist zones and finishing zones combined. The majority of goals and assists will occur in particular areas, and in particular ways. The following diagrams illustrate how some of these zones and actions have combined on the pitch. There are hundreds of thousands of other examples in existence, with new examples being created every week.

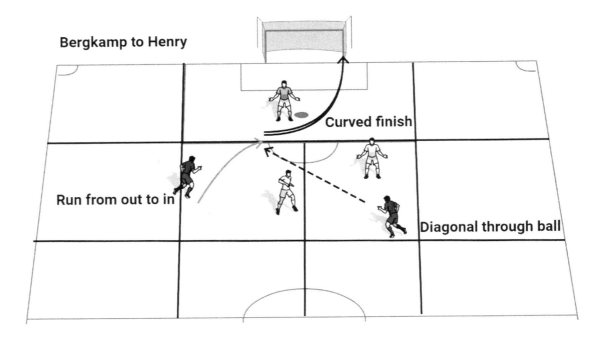

Bergkamp to Henry

Curved finish

Run from out to in

Diagonal through ball

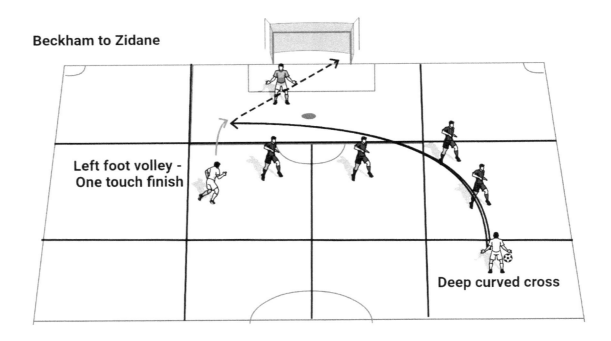

Beckham to Zidane

Left foot volley -
One touch finish

Deep curved cross

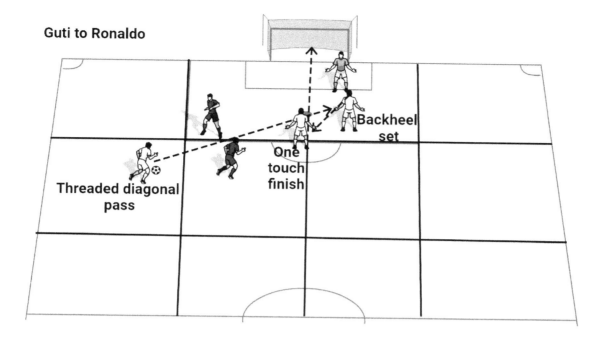

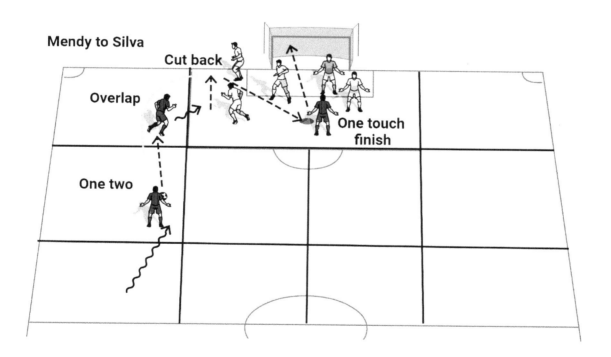

When finishing is being practised, it is important to remember that we are also giving opportunities to develop other techniques. Particularly passing. Another definition we could use for passing and shooting is ball striking. Both actions require very similar techniques. The ability to judge height, speed, and distance will dictate the success of both a pass and a shot. For one technique, we are aiming to hit a player or put the ball within the reach of a player. For the other, we are aiming to miss a player, or put the ball beyond the reach of a player.

These practices also provide opportunities for goalkeepers to thrive. While it is more important than ever for goalkeepers to be effective with the ball at their feet, they also need chances to make saves. Not only for the sake of practising, but also because they love doing it. Goalkeepers enjoy practices in which they are highly active. While they will accept having little to do in games, they will only accept it for so long during practices. We need to bring them to life just as much as our other players.

Finishing and Goalkeeping 1

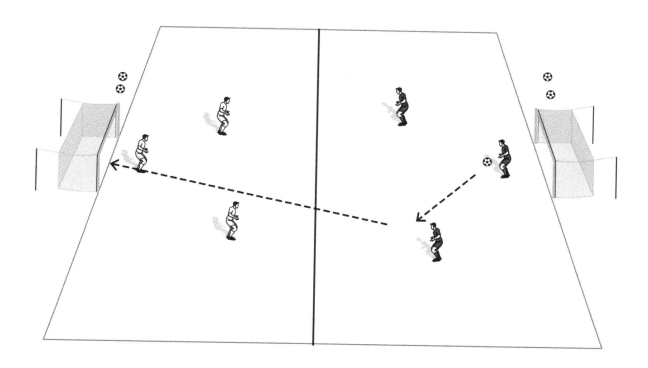

White versus stripes. Teams are locked into their halves, and cannot enter the opposition's half.

Progression 1

One player from each team is locked in the opposition's half.

Progression 2

Players are allowed to enter the opposition half if they have passed into their teammate.

Points

- Touch to set up the shot
- Types of finish
- Shot stopping
- Shot power
- Distribution for goalkeeper

Finishing and Goalkeeping 2

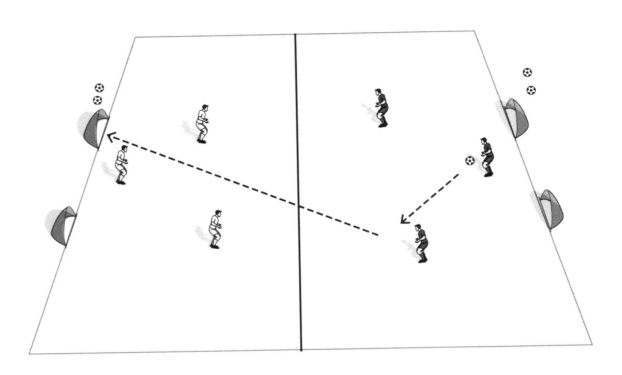

White versus stripes. The mini goals should be close enough to be covered by a goalkeeper. Five points if a team can score in the mini goal, one if the ball passes through the space between the two mini goals. Shoot from own half only.

Progression 1

One player from each team is locked into the opposition half.

Progression 2

Players are free to move anywhere.

Progression 3

Allow the goalkeeper to score with a throw.

Points

-   Touch to set up a shot
-   Positioning to block
-   Types of finish
-   Awareness for goalkeeper
-   Shot stopping
-   Distribution and ball striking for the goalkeeper

Fly 3v3

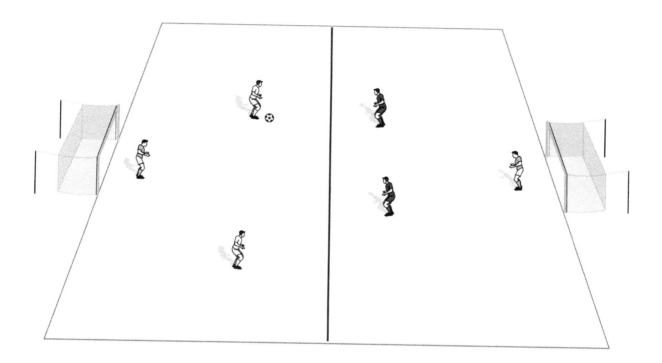

All players are free to move anywhere.

One goal = 1 point

All players, including the goalkeeper, need to be in the opposition's half when a goal is scored. A goal is worth 2 points

If the goalkeeper scores from own half = 2 points

If the goalkeeper scores in the opposition half = 3 points

Progression

The goalkeeper only has four seconds in possession when in their own half

Points

- Freedom for the goalkeeper
- Width and support
- Forward runs
- Long shots

Play! 1

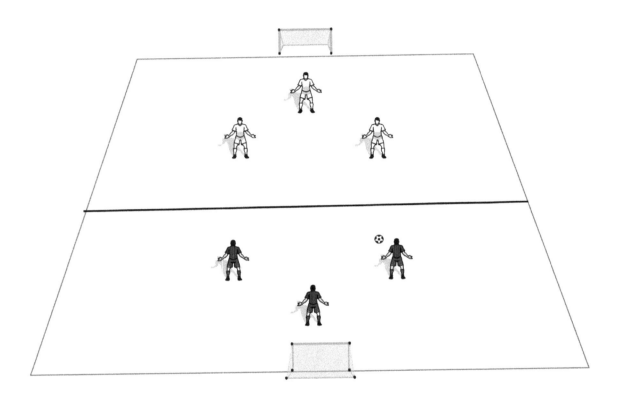

A regular 3v3 game. However, if a player crosses the halfway line (dribbles or passes into another player) the team is now able to attack both goals.

Variation

Play with two mini goals at each end

Points

- Awareness
- Disguise
- Imagination
- Communication
- Transition

Play! 2

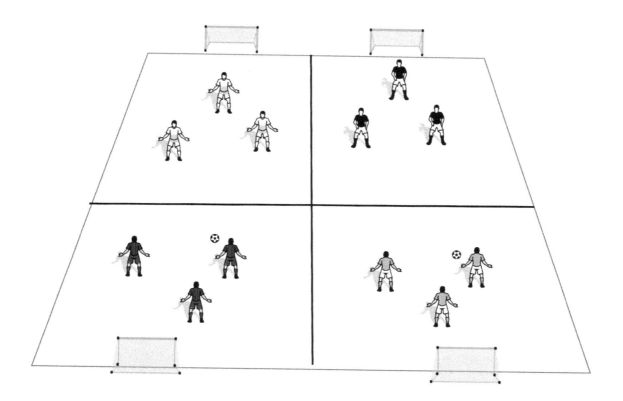

Two separate games to begin with, both working with the rules from Play! 1.

Move on to the rules of Play! 2.

Players can cross any line to open up different goals to attack. If their pass or dribble breaks two lines (diagonal pass or dribble) it will open up more scoring options. For example, if a stripe player only breaks the sideline to the right, they will be able to attack either goal at the top end. However, if they break the side and halfway line, they open up all four goals to attack.

Three Player Finishing

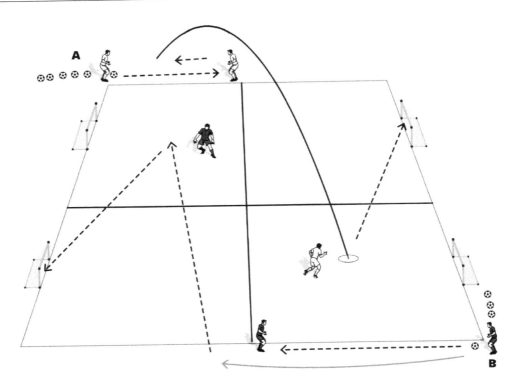

A – The first player passes the ball into his teammate who sets the ball back. The ball is now crossed for a finish into either mini goal. Service can be high or low.

B – The first player overlaps before crossing low for a finish.

Progressions

- For an opposed practice, play from both ends and have the player who sets the ball, or passes for the overlap, quickly recover to mark/pressure the player who is finishing
- Add a goalkeeper. Either move the mini goals closer, or only play with one larger goal at each end.
- Should the goalkeeper or defender gain the ball, counter attack the opposite end.
- The receiving player can decide to cut in and attack/finish 2v1 (or 2v2 with goalkeeper)

Start opposed or unopposed depending on context.

Points

- Timing of movement and timing of pass/cross
- Communication
- Types of cross and types of finish
- Recovery runs

Up, Back, Attack 1

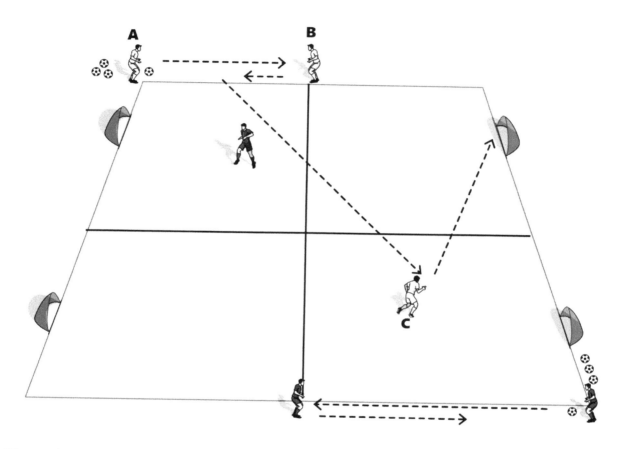

Player A passes into player B. Player B sets to A, who plays into C. Player C finishes into either mini goal.

Begin with a low service to finish. Progress to clipped or chipped service to bring out headers/volleys etc.

Points

- Movement
- Body shape
- Timing

Up, Back, Attack 2

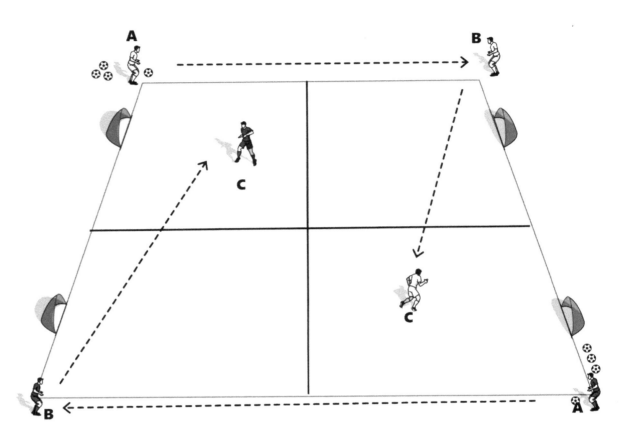

Player A passes into player B, who delivers for player C to finish.

Progression 1

Player A makes a forward run for C to set and finish.

Progression 2

Run the practice one at a time, rather than simultaneously; this will allow player A to act as a defender against player C.

Progression 3

Remove the mini goals and add a large goal with a goalkeeper at each end.

Up, Back, Overlap

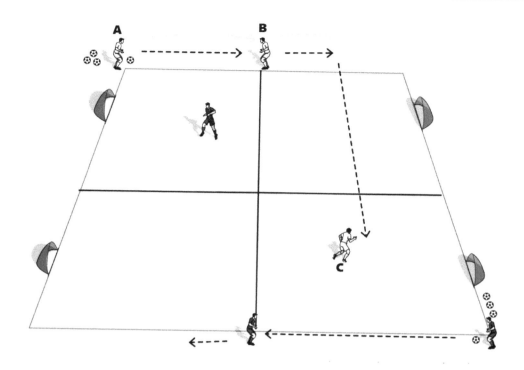

A passes into B. B holds up the ball – as A overlaps – before crossing to C who can score in either of the two mini goals. Vary the service from low to high.

Progression 1

The player who plays the pass for the overlapping player joins the attack to increase the options for the overlapping player.

Progression 2

The player who 'sets' then makes a recovery run to apply pressure to player C

Progression 3

Instead of overlapping, player A makes an underlap inside the pitch.

Progression 4

Replace the mini goals with a large goal. Add a goalkeeper.

Points

- Timing of movement
- Body shape
- Type of finish
- Quality of pass

Overlap to Score

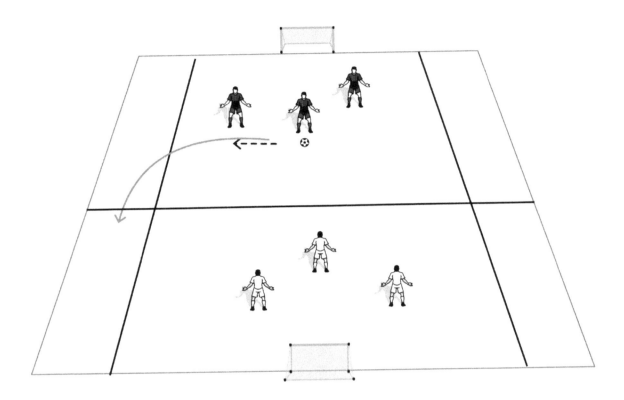

White versus stripe. To score, the ball must be in the opposition's half. If a goal is scored from the central area, that goal is worth one point. If the goal is scored from the wide channel or the assist comes from the wide channel, the goal is worth three points.

A player may not start in the wide position; the aim is for the player to arrive at approximately the same time as the ball (or after the ball).

Defenders may not enter the wide areas.

Progression

Once the ball is in the wide area, a defender may enter the area.

Points

- Movement
- Timing
- Width

Six Player Finishing 1

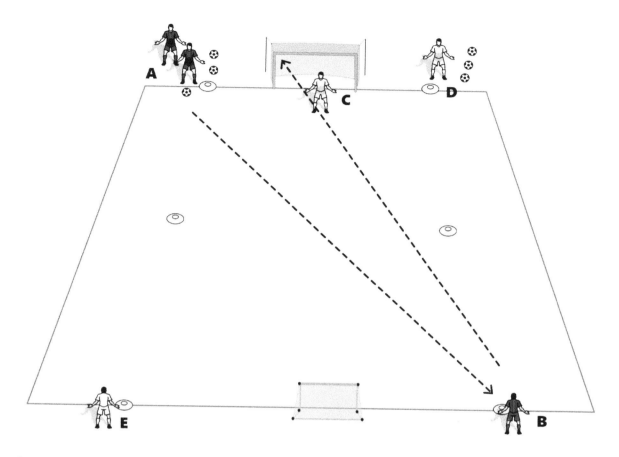

Player A passes to player B. Player B shoots, then takes up position C. The goalkeeper joins position D. Player A goes to position B. Position D passes to E, who then shoots before taking up position C.

If the goalkeeper saves, they can shoot into the smaller goal. The player at position A can look for any rebounds (as can the shooter).

Progression

After passing, player A moves to the middle cone. Player B can pass back to player A if they choose. Both A and B can score. Have a competition between the white and striped teams as to who scores the most goals. Two points if the shot goes straight in. One point for a goal from a rebound or combination with A. If the goalkeeper scores, add a point to their team.

Points

- Quality of pass
- First touch
- Type of finish
- Disguise

Six Player Finishing 2

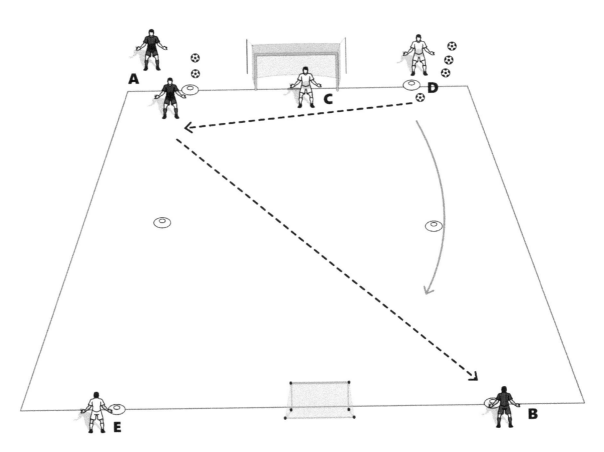

Position D passes to position A. Position A passes to position B. The player from position D moves into a position to defend, as A passes to B. The player in position B can shoot early or face a 1v1 with the defender. Player B will go in goal after the attack. Position A will then pass to position D, who passes to position E, repeating the process.

Progression

Player A and B combine to create a 2v1 against the defender.

Points

- First touch
- Type of finish
- Shift and shoot
- Combination

Combination Shooter

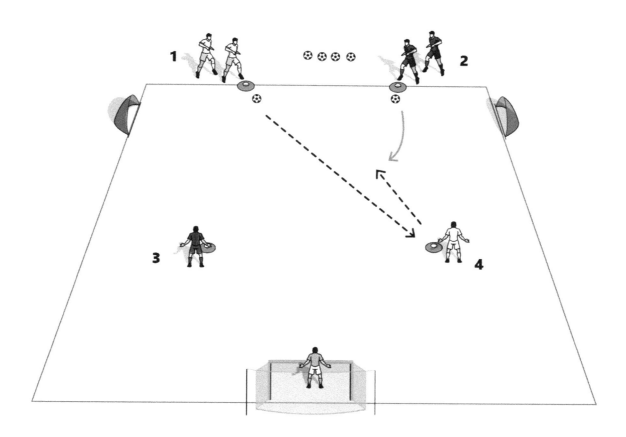

Combination 1

Player 1 passes into player 4 who sets the ball back to player 2. Player 2 can finish in any way they choose (dribble to the GK, first-time shot, etc). Then, they return to the position they started in. The player in position 2 passes into position 3 who sets for position 1 to finish. Progress to the setting player applying pressure on the finishing player.

Combination 2

Player 1 passes to player 4 who sets to player 2. Player 2 passes to 3 who needs to read the movement of player 2. Player 4 defends against player 2 and player 3 in a 2v1. Player 2 may decide to make a run around the outside to overlap, or run straight through the centre. Should player 4 decide to track player 2 – and apply no pressure to player 3 – player 3 may finish.

Combination Shooter (cont)

Progression 1

Player 1 may also recover to make a 2v2 + the goalkeeper.

Progression 2

The remaining players at position 1 and 2 also join to create a 3v3 + the goalkeeper.

Any defender who wins or regains possession, may attack either of the two mini goals.

Points

- Movement
- Overlap
- Underlap
- Set and spin
- Straight pass, diagonal run
- Types of finish
- Element of transition

Working with the Forward

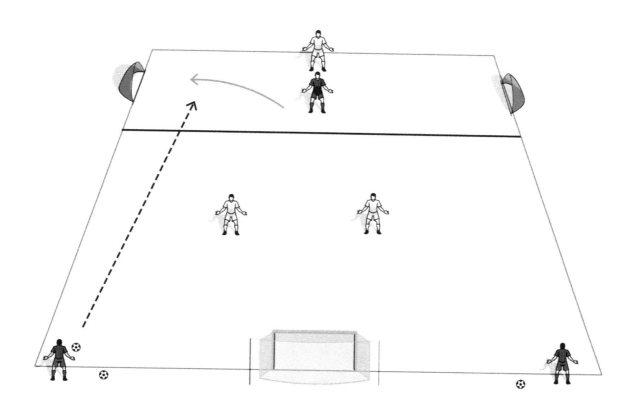

One stripe and one white are locked into the zone with the two mini goals. The stripes near the large goal play into the stripe locked in with the white. The stripe forward works to find space and score in either of the mini goals.

The two white players in the middle try to front screen and prevent the pass into the forward. If they intercept, they can score in the large goal. If no direct pass is on, the stripes may pass to each other to shift the whites.

Progression 1

Move the stripes from the line, and allow them to move freely in their area.

Progression 2

The forward can rotate with a teammate to vacate space and enable another player to find space in the forward zone. The defender remains locked in.

Working with the Forward (cont)

Progression 3

Allow the defender to track the forward when the player decides to drop out of the zone. A central white can follow a forward run into the zone.

Points

- Movement to create passing lines
- Use of body to protect the ball or turn the defender
- Movements to deceive the defender
- Rotation
- Communication
- Triggers

Target Man 1

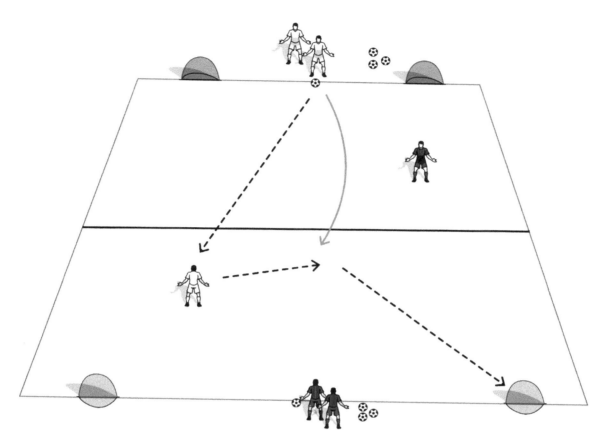

Each group has a player locked into one half of the area; that participant is the target player. The target player lays the ball off to the player who passed the ball in, who then finishes into a mini goal.

One group plays at a time, with the target player making movements to create a line for the pass.

Progression 1

Both groups play at the same time, making it harder for the target man to find a good passing line.

Progression 2

Vary the type of service into the target player.

Target Man 1 (cont)

Progression 3

The stripes and the whites play against each other with one middle player acting as the target player when their team is passing in, and the other acting as the defender. Can they combine with their teammate or spin the defender to score?

Points

- Quality of pass
- Which side of the target player are we looking to play to?
- Movement to find/create space
- Use of the body to hold off the defender
- Movement to support

Target Man 2

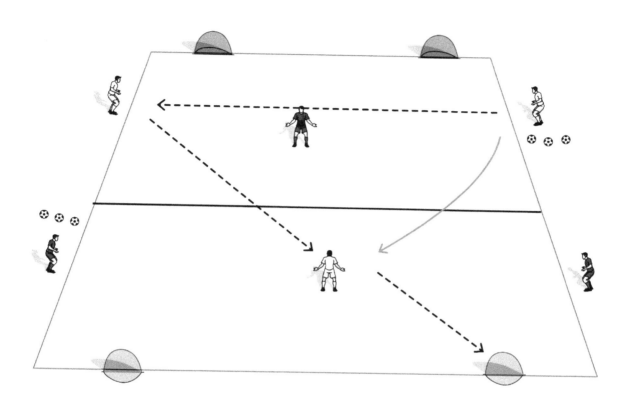

A pass is played square before being fed into the forward, who sets for a finish.

Progression 1

When the ball is played in, the two players positioned at the side become active defenders to create a 2v2 attack. If the defenders win the ball, they counter attack.

Progression 2

The other players join to create a 3v3 with a recovery run, and a run from deep (or act as deep-lying support). If the defenders win the ball, they counter attack.

Points

  - Quality of pass
  - Movement to find space
  - Cutting in
  - Forward runs
  - Combinations

Left v Right 1

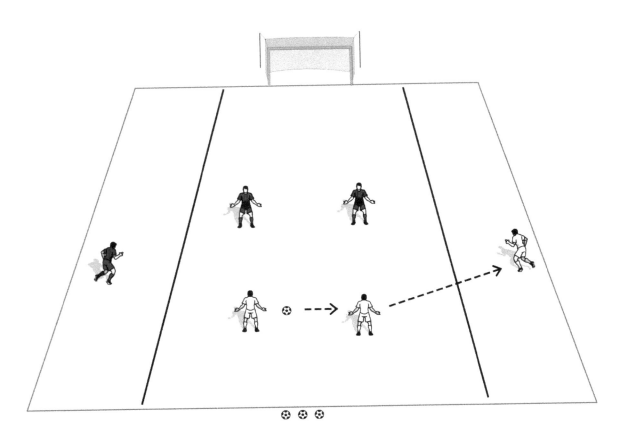

Two versus two in the centre. Whites have a right-footed player in the right-hand channel. Stripes have a left-footed player in the left-hand channel.

The team in possession can combine through the middle to score without using the wide player; however, there is always going to be an overload available. Should the stripes regain possession, they pass to their wide player in the channel to reset the attack (whites defend the one goal).

With a right-footer on the right, and a left-footer on the left, the most likely move is for the player to drive to the line and cross or hit an early cross.

The addition of a shooting line may aid the practice.

Progression 1

Allow the wide player to score with a one-touch finish. Does this challenge the positioning of the defenders?

Left v Right 1 (cont)

Progression 2

Place a left-footed player on the right, and a right-footed player on the left. The wide player may cut in, and their closest teammate takes up the position in the wide channel.

Progression 3

Add a goalkeeper

Points

- Movement
- Combinations
- How can the two central players create more time/space for the wide player?
- Types of cross
- Types of finish

Left v Right 2

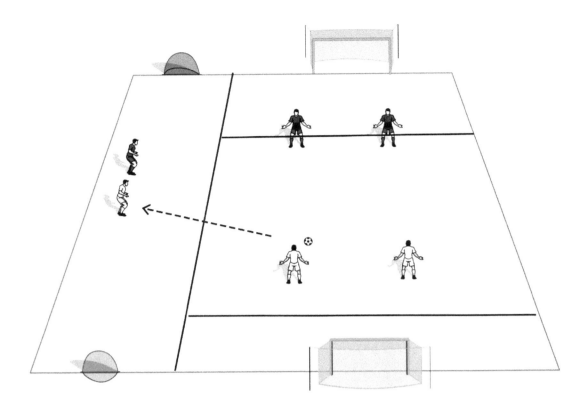

Two versus two on the main pitch. The players can score once they are within the shooting line. On the right is a 1v1 set up where the two players play against each other. They score in either the mini goals or the large goal.

Progression 1

Once the wide player has touched the ball, all players can score from anywhere.

Progression 2

A goal can be scored from the middle zone for one point. If the wide player scores in a 1v1, it is worth two points. If a one-touch finish is scored from inside the shooting line, the goal is worth two points.

Progression 3

If a goal is scored from a cross, it is worth three points.

Progression 4

The wide player can cut inside, but a central player must rotate out to take their place.

Four Zero

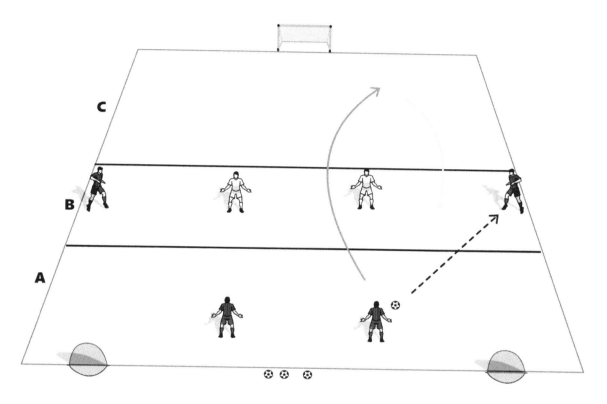

Play begins in zone A. After a pass, whoever has played the pass makes a forward run through zone B and into zone C. If there is no forward pass into zone C, the player who made the run loops back through zone B into any space vacated by a player who has made a forward run.

Score with a one-touch finish in zone C. Defenders may recover into zone C or track the run into C. If the defenders win the ball, they can attack the mini goals in zone A.

Progression 1

Add a number of passes before being able to play the killer pass.

Progression 2

Allow defenders to press into Zone A.

Progression 3

Add a goalkeeper if available. Remove the one-touch finish rule.

Four Zero (cont)

Progression 4

Allow shots from zone B.

Points

- Encourage forward runs
- Use one-twos and parallel passes
- Encourage wide players to break forward when the ball is passed into zone C
- Try to play with a left-footer on the right, and right-footer on the left, to create different passing possibilities.

Long Shot

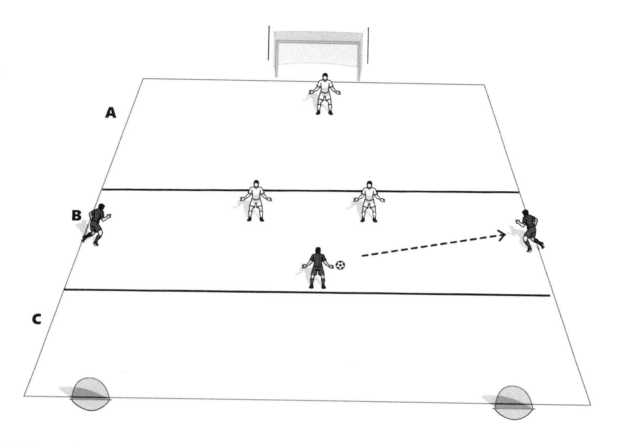

All the stripes, and two whites, are locked into zone B. The goalkeeper is locked into zone A. Stripes score in the large goal, whites score in the two mini goals. Stripes take advantage of the 3v2 to create a shooting chance. Whites look to score when they regain possession.

Progression 1

The white team can break into zone C to score. Stripes may track them to regain possession.

Progression 2

Stripes can break into zone A to score.

Progression 3

Stripes scoring system C=3, B=2, A=1. Whites scoring system A=3, B=2, C=1.

Chapter 6

Long Shot (cont)

Points

- Angles and distances
- Fast ball movement
- First touch to set up a shot
- Draw players in to create more space for others
- Types of finish

Transfer and Finish

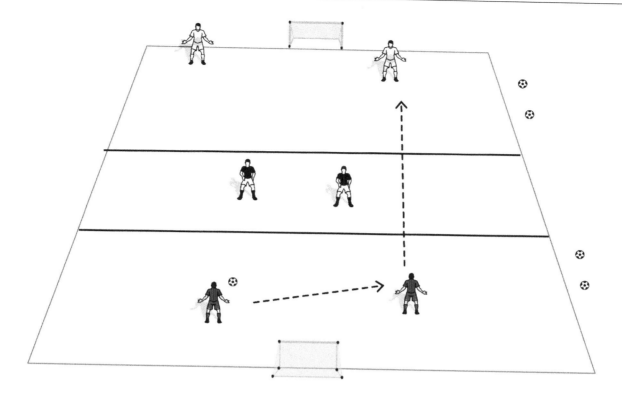

Stripes try to play across to whites without the black team intercepting. Whites then try to play across to the stripes. If the black team intercept, they can attack the goal of the team who lost the ball. If the team are able to score, switch.

Progression 1

If the ball is played across, the player who passes follows his pass for a set and finish. The player who did not receive the ball, moves to the other side to create rotation.

Progression 2

Allow the middle players to leave their area and press.

Progression 3

Add goalkeepers.

Points

- Patience and Awareness
- Angles
- Positioning
- Movement

Positional Defend and Attack

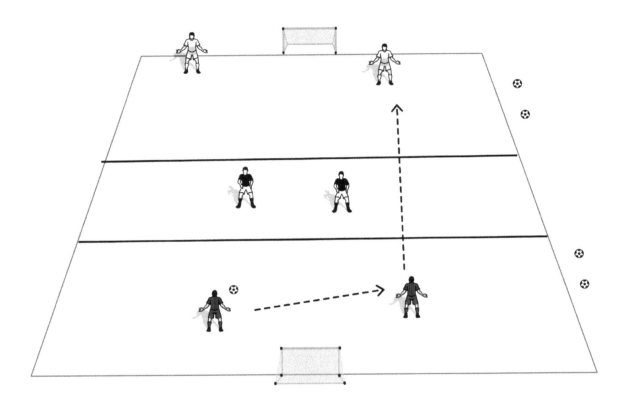

Play starts with the middle player in row C passing to either the left or right. The next pass goes into one of the players in row B, who attacks the goal. Row A acts as defenders. Row C sits back to provide support.

After five attacks, row A moves to C. C moves to B. B moves to A.

How can B attack? What methods might they use?

Progression 1

Allow row C to fully join the attack.

Progression 2

Add goals for the players in row A to attack if they regain possession.

Positional Defend and Attack (cont)

Points

- Use the initial pass to trigger movements from forwards (for example, central player pushes higher, wide players move wider)
- Combinations
- One-twos
- Overlaps
- Underlaps
- Deep crosses/low crosses/diagonals
- Through balls
- Cut in and shoot
- Tempo of attack

The Condition Game

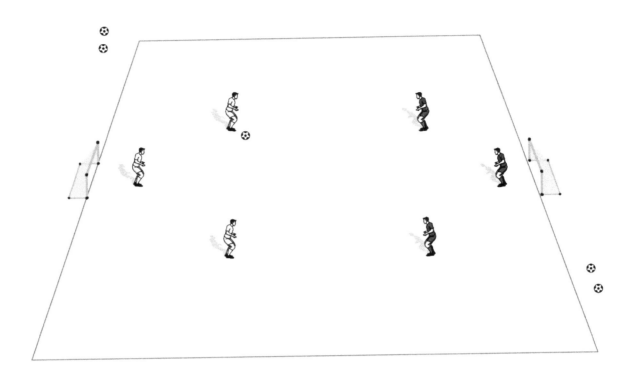

A 3v3 game played in a small area. Small enough that the GK can shoot and score from their own goalmouth.

When a player scores, the scoring team chooses an opponent to remove from the pitch and add one goal to their score. If the team is already a player down, they can either bring their player back onto the pitch, or take an opponent off, while also adding a point to their team's score. If a team removes all the opposing players from the pitch, add a bonus goal as well as the point for the goal scored. All players then return to the pitch.

Progression

Instead of a player leaving the pitch, the team they score against can place a condition on the opposition (e.g., they can only score with a one-touch finish, they are not allowed to tackle, etc.). If a team scores, they can choose to remove the condition or add a condition to the opposition.

This game can be taken seriously; utilise the conditions that might technically, or tactically, help players. Or, it can be taken to extremes for pure fun (a player must play with one hand touching the ground at all times, a player must play in the style of crab football, etc.).

Real World

I use the first goalkeeping and shooting practice at one specific session. The ball we have available is very small and it is impractical to play more than 3v3. The session is an hour and a half, and variety is vital. After a lot of trial and error, the goalkeeping and shooting practice proved so popular that the team requested it every week!

While the session did help develop the players' shooting, I also witnessed a dramatic improvement in goalkeeping. Players would *want* to be the goalkeeper because they were always involved in the action, either making saves or taking shots themselves.

By the end of the year, the team had several viable options in goal and the position was immensely popular. Rather than being seen as an afterthought, with the last willing player being pushed into goal, it was a sought-after position.

7
General 3v3

Why 3v3?

A reminder.

Using 3v3 decreases the number of players on the pitch, in order to attain more touches per player, while retaining the minimum number of players possible to enable width and depth in both attack and defence.

"Strategically, 3v3 football uses the smallest tactical unit able to apply the principle of depth and breadth for effective team offence and defence." From *Effective 3-A-Side Game Formats And Team Strategies For Advanced Level* by Harry Hubball, Ian Franks, Mike Sweeney, and Risto Kauppinen.

Technical Actions	3-a-side	4-a-side	5-a-side	Bout 1	Bout 2	Bout 3
Involvements with the ball	31±6	32±4	31±4	33±4	31±5	30±4
Passes	19±4	20±4	22±4	20±3	20±4	19±3
Target passes (%)	73.4±9	75±11	76±9	75.4±6	75.1±8	74±11
Crosses	3±1	1±1	1±1	2±1	2±1	1±1
Dribbling	4±2	2±1	2±1	3±1	3±2	3±1
Shots on goal	3±1	2±1	2±1	2±1	2±1	2±1
Tackles	2±1	2±1	2±2	2±1	2±1	2±1
Headers	1±1	1±1	1±1	1±1	1±1	1±1

± Calculated on 2 sessions

Table from the paper *The Usefulness Of Small-Sided Games Training* by Filipe Manuel Clemente, Micael S. Couceiro, Fernando Manuel Lourenco Martins and Rui Mendes.

The table above shows the number of technical actions per game when small-sided games are used. The numbers, in general, are very similar. The information not displayed is the number of actions per player, but simple maths can determine that six players having 31 involvements with the ball will have around 5 involvements each while ten players with 31 involvements/passes will have around 3 involvements each.

Chapter 7

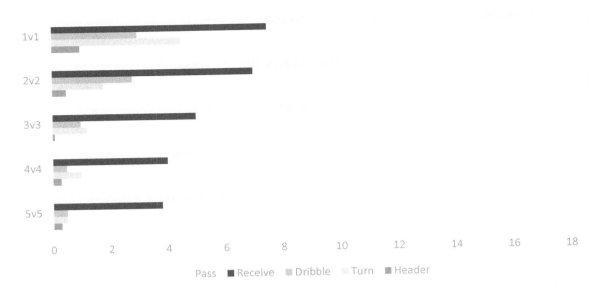

"An increase in the number of players performing led to an increase in the total number of technical actions performed. However, the addition of extra players also led to a decrease in the total number of technical actions performed per player." *From Small-Sided Games: The Physiological And Technical Effect Of Altering Pitch Size And Player Numbers* by Adam Owen, Craig Twist and Paul Ford.

In my first book, I very deliberately left area sizes out of all the diagrams. This decision was made because the practices should be equally useful for an under-6 player, as for an under-18. However, the same practice may need to take place on a different-sized area for under-18s and under-6s, in order to fit their physical needs. The aims of the practice will not have changed; just the area operated within. The size of the area may need to be different for one group of under-7s to another group of under 7-s based on their physical development.

A further complication may be the outcome we are looking for with the players. For example, smaller areas may be utilised to encourage more technical individual work, pressing, or more shooting; conversely, larger areas may be used to encourage higher physical returns, running with the ball, or counter-attacking opportunities. The same practice may be changed quite radically by elongating or widening an area. Practices with an emphasis on pressing could have greater 'success' for passing players by enlarging the space, as it increases the challenge for pressing players. Area size will also impact the number of game actions. For example, a larger area is more likely to decrease the number of shots and increase the number of headers.

In a footballscience.net article, the sizes of areas were outlined based on the number of players involved, in comparison to the square metres covered, working from 1v1 up to 10v10.

Number of players	General pitch area (metres)	Small	Medium	Large	Pitch area (metres squared)
1v1	10x10	5x10	10x15	15x20	100
2v2	20-28x20-21	10x15	15x20	20x25	400-800
3v3	**25x18**	**12x20**	**15x25**	**18x30**	**240-2500**
4v4	30-40x20-30	16x24	20x30	24x36	240-2208
5v5	32-62x23-44	20x28	25x35	30x42	240-2500
6v6	49x37	24x32	30x40	36x48	240-2500
7v7	50x35-45				875-2200
8x8	60x40-45				2400-2700
9v9	60x50				3000
10v10	90x45				4000

For the purposes of this book (and indeed the first book), we might consider small as an area designed for the foundation phase (5-11), medium as an area designed for the youth development phase (12-16), and large as an area designed for the professional development phase (17 and up). As suggested previously, considerations will need to be made based on the needs of a specific group or aims of a practice. A medium area may be appropriate for a foundation phase group if we are looking to encourage more running with the ball. A small area may be appropriate for a professional development phase group if we are encouraging protecting the ball and turning.

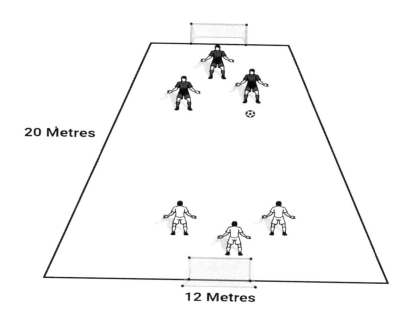

20 Metres

12 Metres

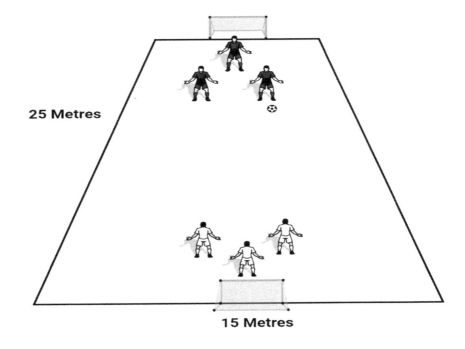

25 Metres

15 Metres

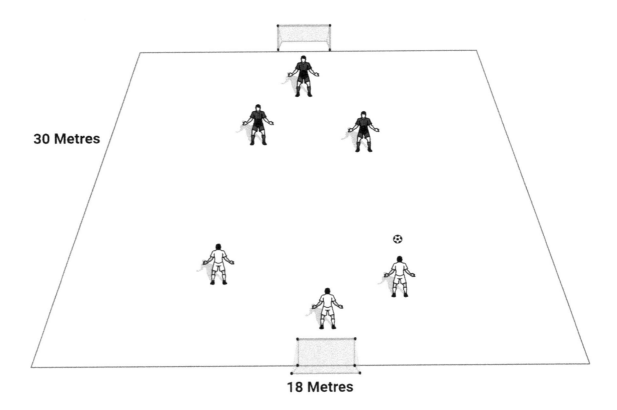

30 Metres

18 Metres

Before selecting area sizes and choosing our depth of detail, we have to understand what the purpose of the session is. Context is crucial. As a grassroots coach, the likelihood is that players – no matter what their age – are more likely to want to play than to train. Even at higher levels, players are more likely to want to play than train. Your session with these players could be their only opportunity to play football that week. Or it might be one out of 20 football sessions they attend.

Those two examples might exist within the same group. Our challenge is to provide an opportunity for all players to get what they need, *and* what they want.

As well as leaving out area sizes, the level of detail on most of the session designs are relatively low. The reason for this is to allow space for the sessions (and players) to breathe. Practice design is influenced by so many elements. Players need opportunities to practice and opportunities to play. Somewhere amongst those opportunities, there also needs to be repetition/exploration of technique and decision making. Players also need the opportunity to be helped by their coach.

High detail levels are fantastic for specific outcomes but often – by having very specific outcomes – the learning opportunities for players become narrow. The possible solutions become finite, rather than infinite. By leaving blank spaces, the players are free to fill them in the manner that they feel is best – be that in the moment, or through a pre-planned solution. As coaches, we may have several possible alternatives for the players should they require them. There is every chance that, between them, the players will have more solutions than the coach! We can plan for their ideas by leaving breathing space. The space to experiment, the space to question, the space to think, the space to reflect.

The practice design and conditions are our co-coaches, and they help the players reach their potential. Can we draw out their knowledge and understanding? Or are players empty vessels for coaches to pour their knowledge into? Transference of knowledge would seem to be a logical process, passing on our experiences for their benefit. There are problems with this outlook, though. Whomever we are, our knowledge will have limits. Which is not to say that our knowledge will not be useful (there will certainly be times when it is), but there are many more sources of knowledge available to our players than just us. One of those sources of knowledge can be the players themselves, aiding their individual development with new solutions or aiding the development of their peers by sharing their ideas. All of this is about the future. Building a better future for the players. As the cliché goes, children are the future; *their* ideas and experiences will help shape how *they* perceive football.

If the path young players are sent down takes them towards a form of binary football, where A must equal B, we are a party to the creation of a limited game. However, should the players be able to see how many options there are, that A might = B, C, D, E, or F (or even more), the future of the game will be more intelligent, versatile, and flexible. Football may stay – relatively-speaking – the same and recognisable, but tactics and game models will change. Even rules will change. Players need to be prepared to cope with change.

Football is complex, but it is not complicated. It is simple because the objective of the game is to score more goals than the other team. It is complex because of the massive number of ways this can occur, mixed with the massive number of ways in which we can prevent this happening. Added to this are the variables of individuals behaving in unpredictable ways. This means that a simple plan can be highly complex, while a complicated plan with set movements is less complex. High levels of complexity require decision making in order to find solutions. Narrowing the possibilities may help find specific outcomes, but the challenge will always be to direct practice in a specific direction while avoiding A must equal B.

"Practicing on smaller pitches, Liverpool were always going to play a short passing game. We only trained with small goals, so there was little long-range shooting. We passed the ball until we were close enough to score. The philosophy centred on passing, making angles, and one-touch football" **John Barnes**

Numbers 1

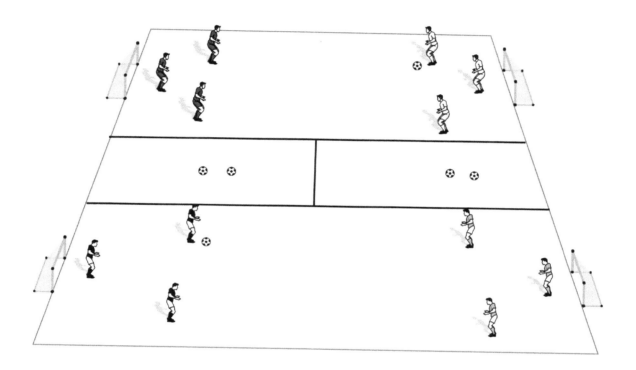

Two 3v3 games. Each player is numbered 1, 2, or 3. When their number is called, they run to one of the footballs and perform a challenge before rejoining their game. Should the players be slow to respond, or slow to complete the challenge, an overload will be created.

Example challenges

- X number of keep ups
- X number of toe taps
- X number of stepovers

The players may come up with their own challenges.

Numbers 2

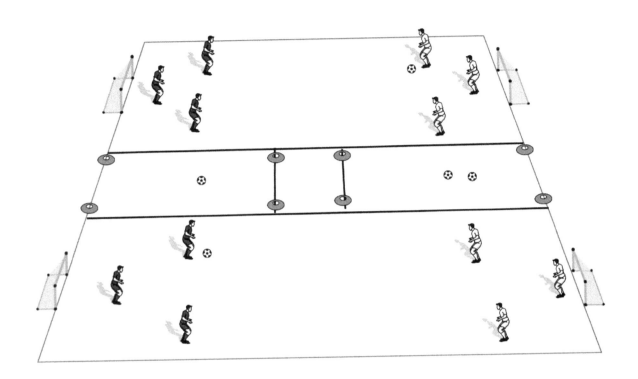

Two 3v3 games. The players are numbered 1, 2, or 3. When their number is called, the players face off in a 1v1 in the centre against a player from the opposing side. The player who wins their 1v1 adds one point to their team's score.

Progression 1

The player who loses has to perform a challenge before they can rejoin their game (keep ups, etc.)

Progression 2

After completing the 1v1, and the challenge, the players join the opposing team (e.g., stripe joins white)

Points

- Overloads
- Communication
- Organisation

Cross Purpose

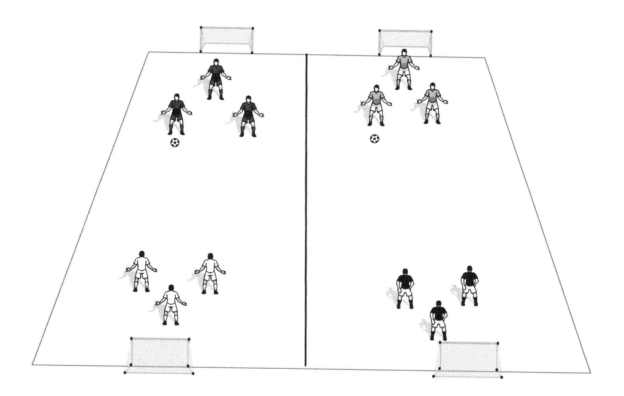

Normal 3v3 games with stripes playing whites, and green playing black.

Progression 1

Whites play green, and stripes play blacks (e.g., the matches become diagonal). The teams do not move goal; they play 'across' the area and through the interference.

Progression 2

Whites play black, and stripes play greens. Again the teams do not move from their positions. The matches are now lateral, with the goals at right-angles to the play.

Where is the space? How can players use it? How does this affect the way they attack and defend?

Understanding Space

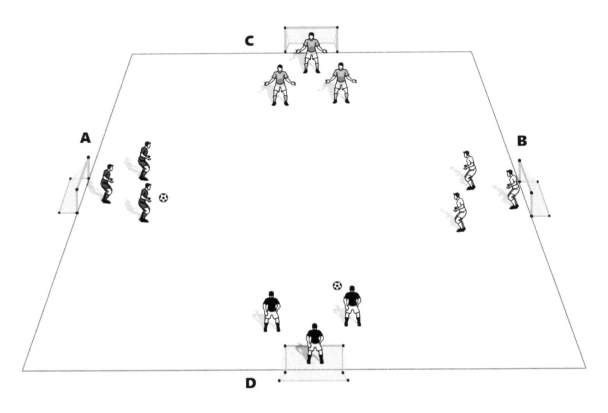

1. A v B and C v D. Heavy interference within the games; awareness will be required.

2. A v C and B v D. The active area between the goals is tight, but there is space available.

3. A v D and C v B. As with 2 but a change of angles. This will affect the types of shot/cross/pass.

4. Chaos 1 – Two balls on the pitch, teams can score in any goal (apart from their own!)

5. Chaos 2 – Four balls on the pitch, teams can score in any goal (apart from their own!)

In games 4 and 5, all sorts of unimaginable outcomes and problems can, and will, occur.

Corner Goals

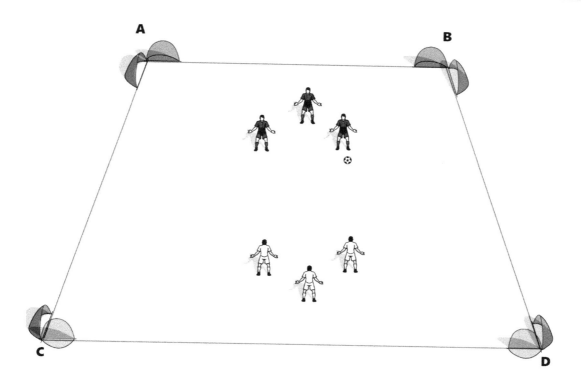

Stripes versus whites. Stripes attack goals A and B. Whites attack goals C and D.

Progression 1

Teams can score in any goal.

Progression 2

The first team to score in all four goals is the winner. Once a team has scored in a goal, they cannot score in that goal again.

Progression 3

The first team to score in all four goals wins; however, a team can score in any goal at any time to add a point to their score. Set a time limit; if no team has scored in all four goals, inside the time limit, the team with the most points wins.

Points

- Use of space
- Fast reactions
- Awareness
- Movement
- Combinations

Play Out

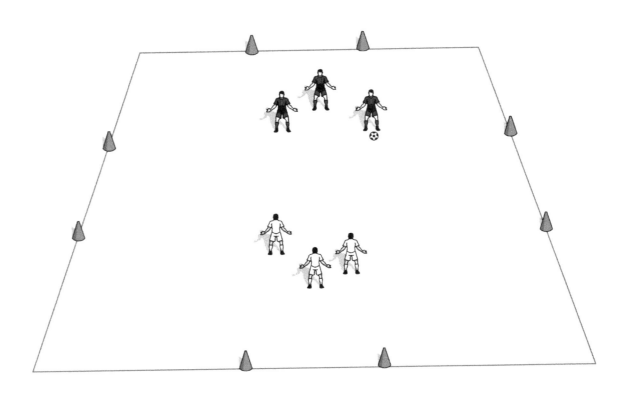

Teams aim to play out through any of the gates. The first team to play through all four gates is the winner. Players may dribble out, or pass to a teammate making a run. Once a gate has been played through, that gate is no longer available to the team who played through it.

Try to ensure that the gates are wide enough so that a whole team cannot entirely block the gate.

Progression 1

Only passes through the gate to a teammate will count.

Progression 2

All gates are available to score in, at all times. Who can score the most points?

Points

- - Understanding and using space
- - Body shape to play forward
- - Awareness
- - Concentration

Three Teams, Three goals

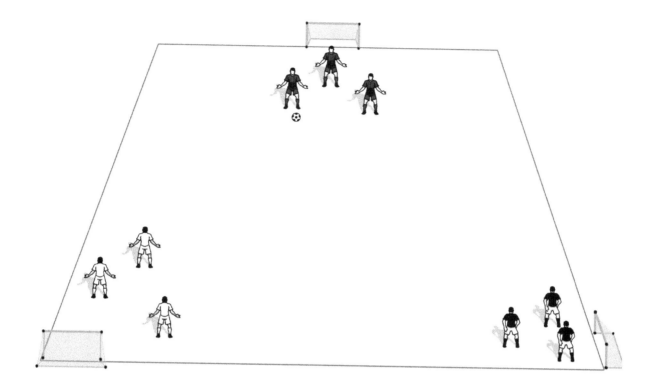

Stripes versus whites versus blacks. Only one ball on the pitch. Space will be hard to come by. If the ball goes out, restart play next to the goal closest to where the ball went out. It will be that team's ball.

Progression

Each team has a ball of their own.

In the first version of the game, finding space will be the challenge as the team in possession will be outnumbered two to one. In the second version of the game, awareness will be the challenge as players will need to keep track of three footballs. (It is possible that all three footballs could be directed towards one goal at the same time.)

Points

- Teamwork
- Communication
- Awareness
- Retain/protect the ball
- Fast attacks
- Awareness

Feel The Pressure

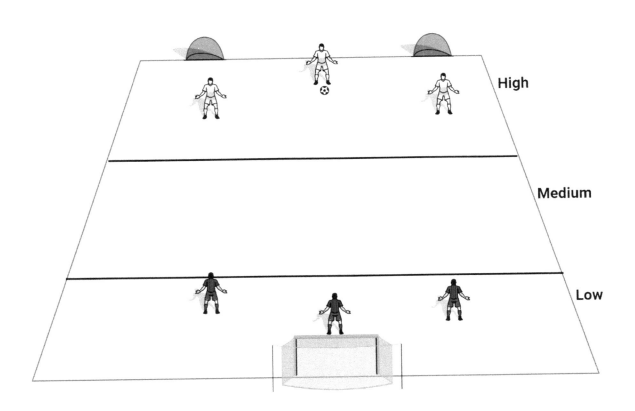

The playing area is divided into three zones. Each zone represents a different pressing area: high, medium, and low. The white team tries to score in the large goal. The stripes aim to regain possession and score in the small goals.

The striped team can select an area to regain possession; should they regain the ball, in that selected area, they score a point. Should they regain the ball and score, they will receive 5 points.

The scoring system can be layered

High = 5, Medium = 3, Low = 1 or High = 1, Medium = 3, Low = 5

Points

- Start position for defending team based on objective
- Body shape
- Angles
- Foot speed
- Cover
- Balance

Pressure plus One

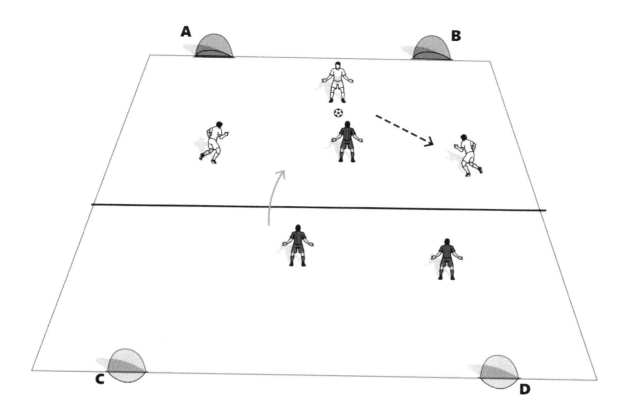

The three white players keep possession against the one striped player. After five passes, the next stripe joins to create a 3v2. After five more passes, the next stripe joins to create a 3v3. Every five passes are worth one point. If the ball goes out of play, it becomes the stripes' turn to keep possession. If the stripes win possession and can get the ball into their area, they start passing immediately with one white going in to press.

Progression 1

When all three defenders are applying pressure, rather than continuing to score points for five passes, the attackers can break out and score in goal C or D for the whites, or goal A and B for stripes.

Progression 2

When the defenders win the ball, they need to score in the goals (A and B for the stripes, C and D for the whites).

Points

- Angles and Distances
- Orientated touch
- Passing techniques

Press/Break Their Line

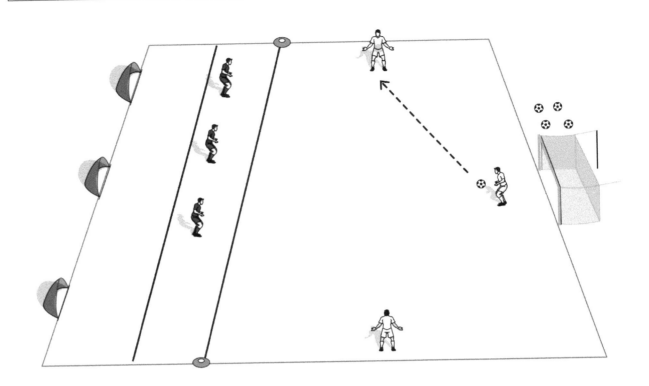

The white team can score in any of the three mini-goals. Stripes can score in the large goal. Play starts with the whites every time. Though the whites have a player close to the goal, that player is not a goalkeeper.

Stripes begin in the channel.

Do the stripes stay back and hold their line or push on and press? If they press, how many press? How many cover?

Do the whites commit all three players to attack or keep a player back to prevent the counter-attack?

Progression 1

Whites can only score from beyond the first line (marked with two red cones). Break the line with a forward pass, forward run, third man run, or dribble.

Progression 2

The white team plays with a fixed goalkeeper.

Progression 3

Add a goalkeeper (4v3)

Three v Three + Three Press

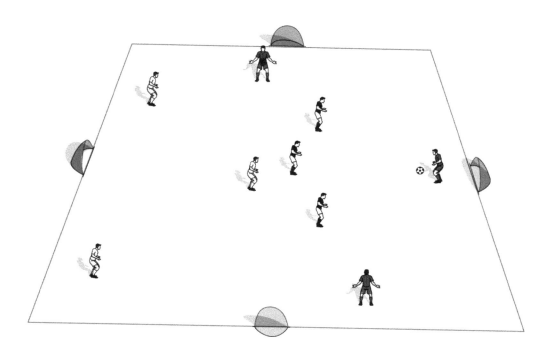

Stripes versus black. The white team helps whichever team is in possession, creating a 6v3.

Progression 1

The team that regains possession needs to score in any of the four mini goals before switching and becoming one of the teams keeping possession. If the goal is not scored, do not switch.

Progression 2

Stripes and whites versus blacks. A timed game with points. Play for two minutes. Five passes by the passing team is a point. For every goal the black team scores, they receive a point. Change roles after two minutes.

Points

- Positioning and use of space
- Transition
- Reaction
- Body shape
- Orientated touch
- Press together
- Make play predictable
- Look for press triggers

Three v One into Three v Two

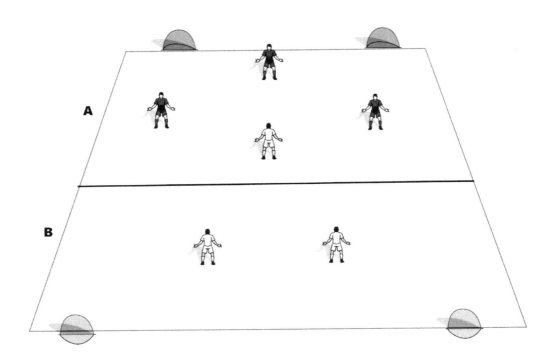

Play starts in zone A with a 3v1. The stripes aim to progress into zone B for a 3v2.

Zone B players cannot enter zone A, but they can position themselves in such a way as to affect the way in which the stripes enter Zone B. The white in zone A cannot enter zone B but may seek to be available for a quick forward pass.

Should the white team win the ball – at any time – they counter-attack; all players may be involved in the counter-attack.

Progression 1

Decide on a set number of passes the stripes need to play before driving forward into zone B.

Progression 2

Start with a 3v2, then move into a 3v1.

Points

- Body orientation and touch orientation
- Dribble/drive with the ball
- Angles
- Speed of pass
- Pressure and distances

Extra Middle Man

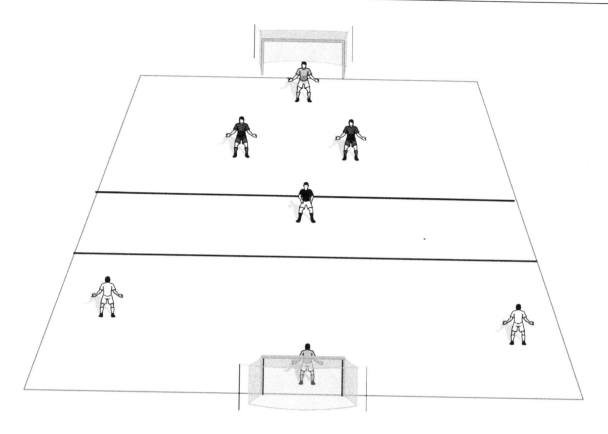

The striped and white players (and the goalkeepers if they wish) can move anywhere in the area. The extra black player is locked into the central area, making him either a target player for counter attacks or a deeper support player if a team has established possession.

If the GK joins the established attack as well, a team could create a 4v2 overload.

Alternative

Play with two mini goals at each end, instead of a single goal, and remove the goalkeepers.

Increase or decrease the size of the central area to adapt the role of the central player in possession.

Points

- Movement
- Support
- Tempo of attack
- Width and depth
- Transition

Play Out or Press

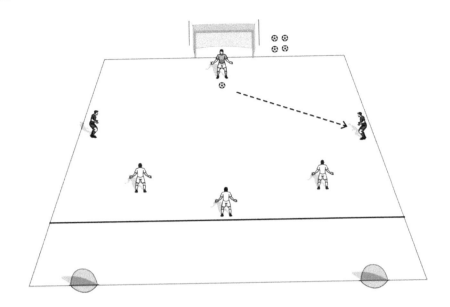

Play starts with the goalkeeper playing to either of his teammates. The stripes attempt to get beyond the shooting line and score in either of the two mini-goals. The whites attempt to regain possession and score.

Progression 1

Allow the stripes to shoot from anywhere (including the goal kick to restart). Does this change the way the whites defend and their start positions?

Progression 2

Allow play to restart from wherever the ball leaves the pitch. Does this change the way the white team presses?

Progression 3

If the stripes and goalkeeper are finding it difficult to restart, allow the goalkeeper to start with a dribble.

Points

- Width and angles
- Safe side for passes
- Orientation of first touch
- Combinations
- Distances (for both attackers and defenders)
- When, where and how to press
- Cover

Goalkeeper Distribution

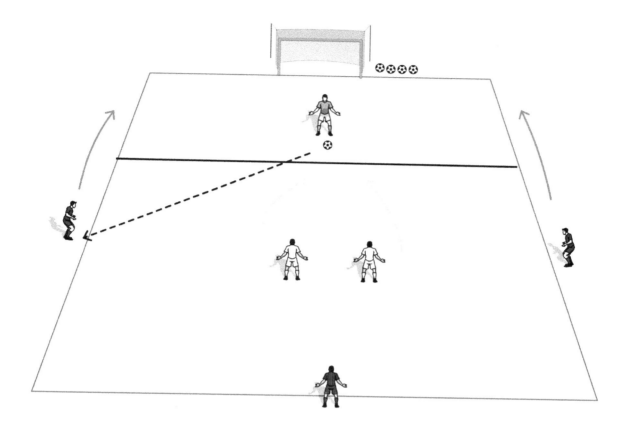

Four versus two.

Play starts with the goalkeeper every time. The stripes look to keep possession. If the white pair win the ball, they attack the goal. The three striped players may leave their line to regain possession and defend.

Points

- Movement is required from the side players and end players to create passing angles.
- The whites need to stop the forward pass and look for opportunities to pressure.
- Use the line as a penalty area for the goal kicks/restarts. The two striped players may drop in to receive the ball; the white players may not enter the area until the stripe has touched the ball (if appropriate to the age of the players).
- First touch
- Fast passes
- Tempo

131

Magic Square – Developed

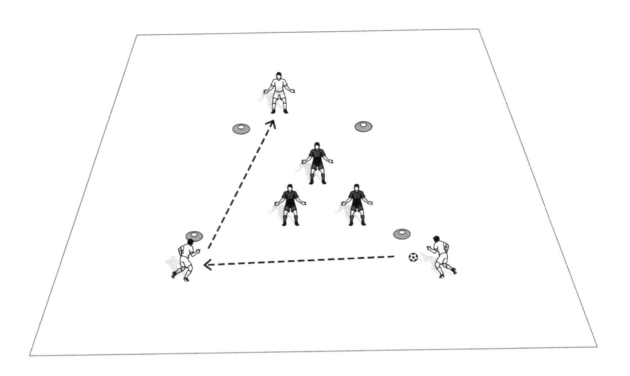

The white team aims to play a pass through the square. The striped team stays organised to stop the pass. Stripes are free to move anywhere around the outside of the square. Stripes are free to organise themselves any way that they choose, within the square, but may not leave the square.

After five attacks, switch roles.

Should the whites consistently move too far from the square, add another square around the square as a boundary.

Points

- Organisation
- Positioning
- Cut out passing lines
- Movement
- Cover
- Balance
- Pressure

Magic Square – Developed 2

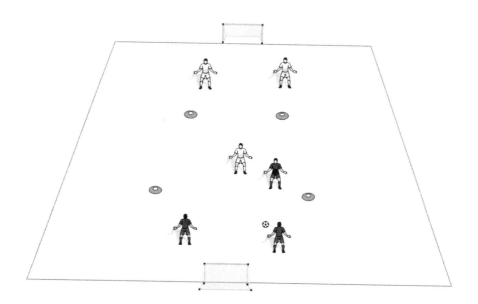

Whites versus stripes. Both teams have a player locked into the central square. A team can score if their central player has received the ball. Once this has happened, all three players able to move freely to score. If a stripe receives the ball, that stripe may leave the area, but the white player must remain.

Progression 1

The defender may leave the area to stay with their opponent.

Progression 2

A goal can be scored at any time, but if the central player is involved in the build-up, the goal is worth two points.

Progression 3

The central player may score from inside the middle area.

Points

- Shielding and turning
- 1v1
- Safe side
- Set
- Overlap
- One-two
- Cutbacks/pullbacks

Release Your Mate

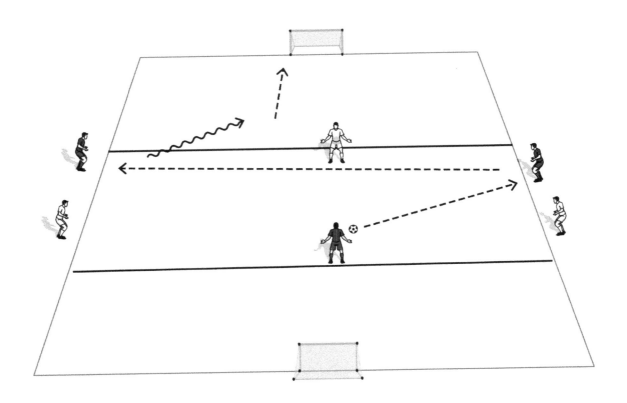

Stripes versus whites.

Each team has one player in the middle and two players on the side. When the player on the outside receives the ball, they are released into the middle. When a team has all three players released, they can attack and score. For the next round, the team that did not score begins with the ball.

Progression

Use the end zones so that a goal can only be scored by a player running onto a through pass.

Points

- Movement
- Combinations
- Forward runs

Front Screen

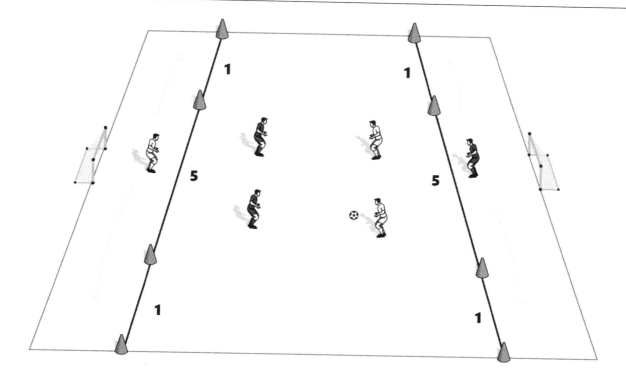

Two versus two in the central area. Both teams have a striker positioned in the respective final thirds. The striker needs to move to receive. If the pass goes through the side gates, the subsequent goal is worth one point. If the pass goes through the central gate, the subsequent goal is worth five points.

Can the defenders position themselves to minimise the points scored?

Progression 1

The forward cannot score; instead, they must look for a set, to an oncoming teammate.

Progression 2

Add goalkeepers.

Points

- Positioning of defenders.
- Distance between the defenders
- Movement of forward
- Forward runs
- Forward passes
- Combinations

Through The Side Gate

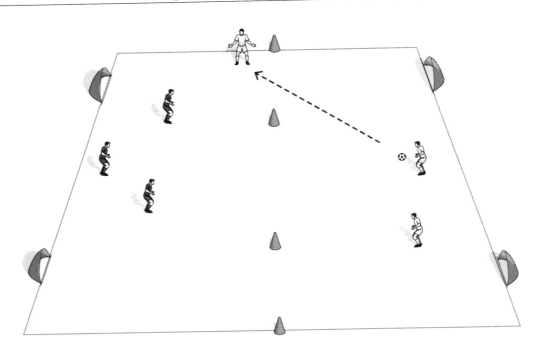

Teams must play through the side gate in order to score in either of the mini-goals. They may get through the gate with either a dribble or pass.

Progression 1

Teams can score in a mini goal at any time, but they will receive bonus points if they play through a side gate before scoring.

Progression 2

Use the centre two cones to form a middle gate. If players play through the central gate, they receive two bonus points.

Progression 3

Remove the mini goals and use one large goal at each end.

Points

- How does the scoring system affect how we position ourselves defensively?
- How does the scoring system affect how we position ourselves offensively?
- Players need to be patient in the build-up to find the opportunity to exploit the sides.
- Players need to be high in the press to stop the passes through.

Aid Possession

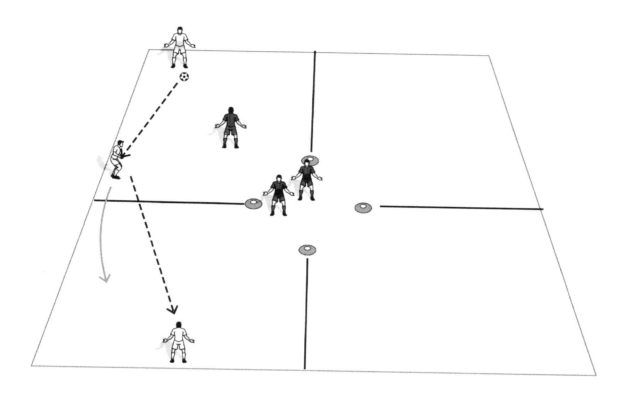

The area is divided into a grid with a secondary area in the centre. The two white defenders occupy one square as a striped defender applies pressure. Two striped defenders wait in the centre.

The third white can move into any of the three empty areas to receive the ball. One of the other two white players moves to support them, while the other occupies a different area. The striped defender returns to the centre, and a different striped player applies the pressure.

If the defending team gains the ball, switch roles.

Progression

Add a number of passes before passing forward.

Points

- Angles
- Distances
- Support
- Movement

Three v Three plus Three Switch

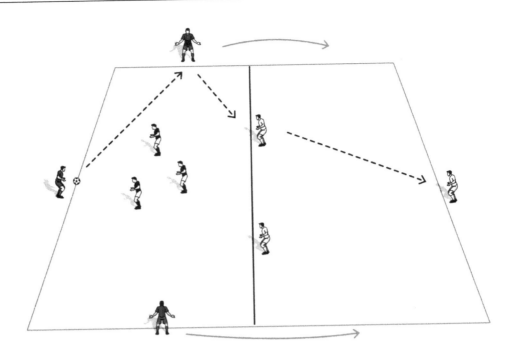

The stripes and whites are in possession. The black team aims to gain possession. If they do get the ball, they switch with whoever lost possession. The aim is to switch the play from one box into the other, with a pass to the target player at each end. Stripes and whites have different roles. The two stripes on the side provide wide support. The two whites in the middle connect the play.

Progression 1

Allow either of the side players to make the switch.

Progression 2

Allow the end players to make the switch.

Progression 3

One of the white central players can move off the line, into the middle, to help possession.

Points

- Movement to support
- Penetrative passes
- Patience and timing
- Body shape
- Orientated first touch

Multi-Area Game

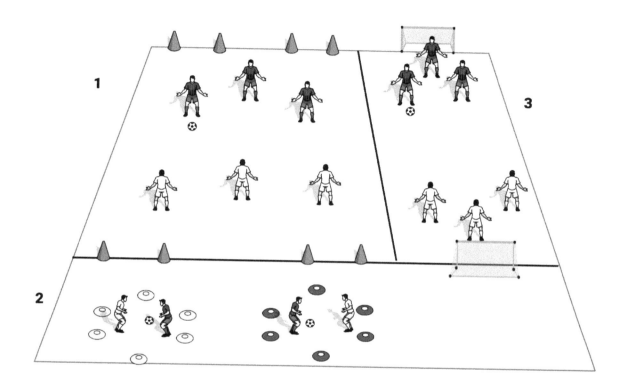

Area 1 – Four-goal game. 3v3 match, dribble through the gate to score.

Area 2 – Two panna games. One point for dribbling through the opponent's gate. Five points for a panna/nutmeg.

Area 3 – Shooting game. Tight area to encourage shots in a 3v3 game.

Two teams split across the areas. The players decide who is playing in which area. At the end of 10 minutes, the teams come together and add up the scores for all of the games. They then choose, again, who plays in the areas but try not to repeat the same players in the same areas.

Commitment, communication, concentration, control and confidence.

Chapter 7

Real World

The numbers game is a classic game played with kids at grassroots clubs, after-school clubs, and summer camps across the UK (and possibly the world). The kids enjoy it, but I am not a fan. The game is often characterised by a high number of players standing and watching while two players have a turn, which may last seconds.

The enjoyable aspect of the game is the 1v1 competition plus team points being available. A number of practices in this chapter achieve both of these elements while avoiding inactive players. In my experience, once players have experienced these games, they never ask to play the numbers game again!

8
Transition

Broadly speaking, football consists of a cycle comprised of four moments. Attack, transition from attack to defence, defence, and transition from defence to attack.

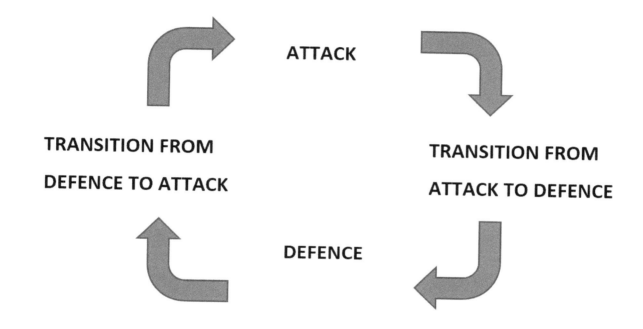

ATTACK

TRANSITION FROM DEFENCE TO ATTACK

TRANSITION FROM ATTACK TO DEFENCE

DEFENCE

Coach education models may deliver these as being: in possession, out of possession, and transition; or we may have a different language that describes transitions as positive or negative. However things are described, we are discussing a change in the state of the game: a change in the directional flow of the game. The quicker we can gain control of a phase of the transition, the more likely it is that our team will succeed.

The control of transition can be achieved in different ways depending on a coach's playing style or game model. Should a team be possession-based, then the sooner that team can regain possession, the more comfortable they should be. Other styles recognise that the moment of transition provides opportunities to exploit temporary disruption as a team seeks to organise itself from an offensive team shape to a defensive team shape (or the reverse). Another method may be to allow the opposition to organise themselves into an offensive shape in the knowledge that possession-based teams create gaps in their own lines as they attempt to stretch the opposition. They look for turnovers closer to their own goal and will then seek a quick vertical transition to attack the gaps left behind.

Chapter 8

"The accent in the counter-attack style lays on the defensive team function, with the emphasis being on the defender's own half of the field and letting the opponents keep the initiative of the game. This is to take advantage of the space behind their defence for their build-up and the attack" **Rinus Michels**

The key to all methods, however, is speed. Though foot speed helps, it is really speed of thought and speed of recognition which are critical. The more opportunities players have to experience transition situations, the better they will be at responding to them. This is only possible if practices have objectives for defending teams and players after they gain possession.

The practices in this book include goals or targets for both sets of players whenever possible (*very rarely is it not possible*). Therefore, all practices contain an element of transition. Yet, like the finishing and creating section, few have transition as the core outcome. The practices in this chapter are dedicated to transition – remembering that transition is not just counter-attacking, it is any moment of turnover or change in the flow of the game that requires offensive or defensive reorganisation. When transition is discussed, it is generally vertical, but arguably the switch of play is a form of a transition (horizontal) which requires both offensive and defensive transition. The lofted horizontal pass is likely to be exploited as the realization that possession has been lost can take longer while the ball hangs in the air. The lofted pass can be a trigger for transition, which may be avoided by keeping passes low.

2v2+2 Transition Rondo

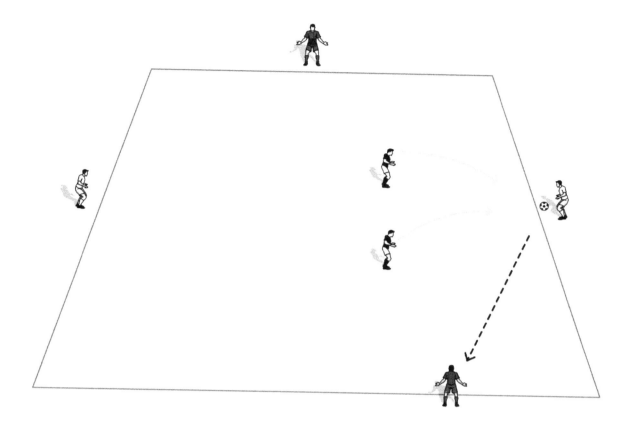

Stripes stay on the ends as support players.

Whites are on the sides.

The middle pair apply pressure.

If the team in the middle regains possession, (either by actually taking the ball at their feet or by forcing a misplaced pass), they aim to take up the positions at the ends (currently occupied by the white pair). The white pair now become the pressing players. The game is always "live" unless the ball goes out of play. Possession may be won back at any time and in any place.

Ensure that the striped team switches roles with one of the other two teams.

Points

- First touch
- Movement to support
- Speed of pass
- Type of pass
- Fast reactions

2v2v2 Transition

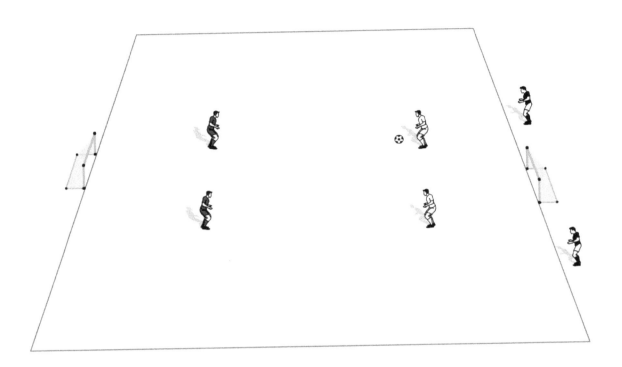

The white team attacks the striped team. When the attack ends (ball off the pitch, in the net, or the stripes win possession), the white team takes a position off the pitch behind the goal they attacked. The striped team then attacks the black-shirted team. When the ball goes off, the black-shirted team attacks the white-shirted team.

Progression 1

Play with one player as the goalkeeper, and one as an outfield player.

Progression 2

Add a shooting line that players must be within in order to shoot (the halfway line or closer to the goal).

Points

- Quick reactions
- Positive intent
- Attack at speed

3v3v3 Transition

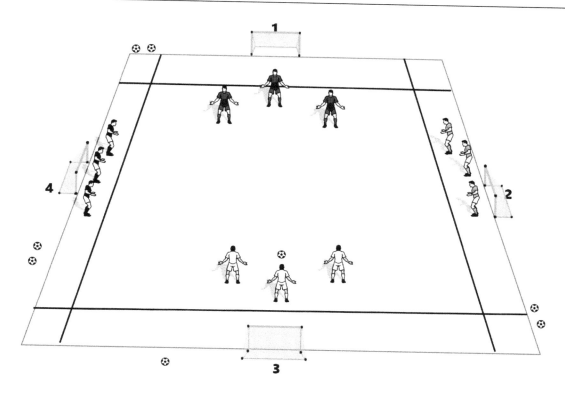

Team 1 starts against team 3. The game is line ball, with a team scoring if they stop the ball inside the opposition's end zone. The game is 'winner stays on'. After either team 1 or team 3 have scored, team 2 will attack them immediately. Whoever scores first in the next game stays on and faces team 4.

Progression 1

The scoring team receives a ball and starts their attack immediately.

Progression 2

Use the goals for 'winner stays on'. A team can only shoot when they have passed into the end zone (enlarge the end zone as needed).

Progression 3

Remove the end zones and shoot at any time.

Points

- Press or drop
- Angles of attack
- Recovery runs
- Recognising danger/opportunities
- Stopping/minimising counter-attacking opportunities

Transfer Check 1

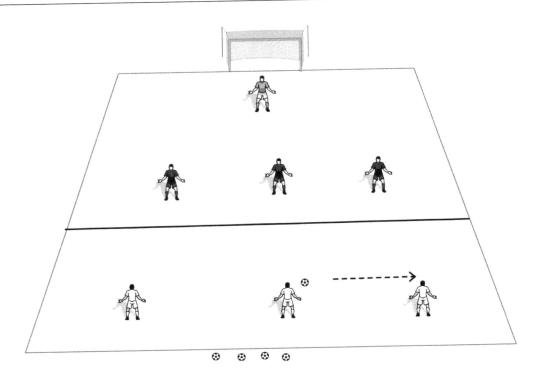

Whites attack against stripes. If the striped team wins possession inside the shooting line (penalty area), they need to get out of the area and then turn and attack the goal they were defending. Players on the white team need to organise themselves quickly, and defend.

Decision for defenders – do they apply pressure high and leave space in behind, or defend deeper knowing it will allow shooting chances and they will have to "check" before they attack? Decision at the turnover – Should the team that lost the ball swarm to regain possession, or concentrate on getting back into position?

Progression

Add a target player near the footballs for the defending team to play into, before they can attack; the attacking team can use them as support.

Points

- Cover
- Balance
- Communication
- Reactions
- Combinations
- Transition
- Awareness

Transfer Check 2

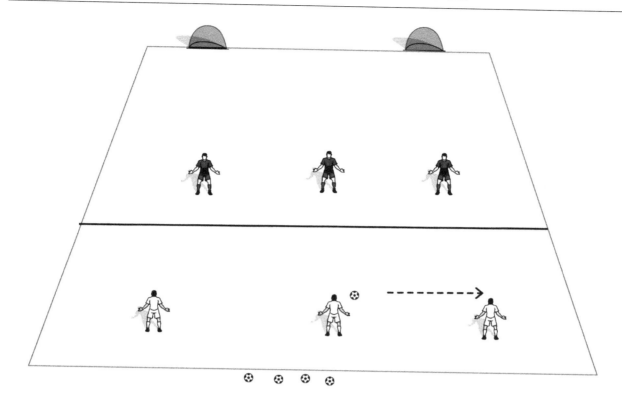

Whites attack against the striped-shirt team. A white player can only shoot once they are past the shooting line (penalty area). Should the stripes regain possession, they must cross the shooting line before turning to attack. However, if the stripes win the ball outside the area, they can attack immediately.

Decision for defenders – do they apply pressure high and leave space in behind, or defend deeper knowing it will allow shooting chances, and they will have to "check" before they attack? Decision at the turnover - Should the team that lost the ball swarm to regain possession, or concentrate on getting back into position?

Progression

Play through a gate (or gates) near the footballs before attacking.

Points

- Cover
- Balance
- Communication
- Reactions
- Combinations
- Transition
- Awareness

Transfer Game 1

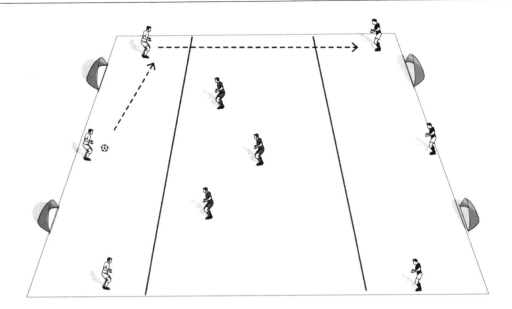

The white team tries to play across to the black team. The stripes try to intercept the ball and, should they succeed, they swap with the team that gave it away.

Progression 1

Ensure that when a teams win the ball, they immediately play to the other side before taking up their position (for example, stripes intercept the ball from the whites, and pass into the black team before taking up their new position). Until the ball has been played across the team who lost it, they cannot attempt to win it back.

Progression 2

The team in the middle can send a player to press.

Progression 3

The team in the middle can send as many players as they like to press. When they win the ball, they can score in either goal. They swap with the team whose goal they scored in.

Points

- Width/shape
- Rapid ball movement
- Splitting passes/looking for gaps
- Cover and balance
- Making play predictable
- Pressing angles

Transfer Game 2

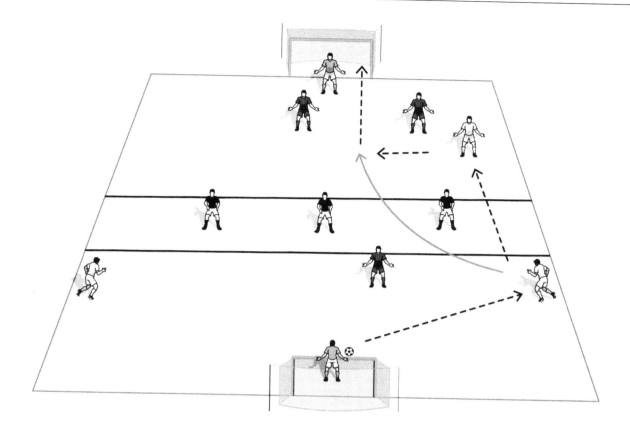

The white team tries to play across – into their target player – without the striped team intercepting in their area, or the black team intercepting in the middle. If the stripes win the ball, they try to play into their forward. If the black team intercepts the ball, they swap with the white team. The goalkeeper is involved in keeping possession and can play across. If the ball is played across, a player can join to create a 2v2 (plus the goalkeeper).

Progression

When the middle team wins the ball, they attack as quickly as possible, keeping the game live unless the ball has gone out of play.

Points

- Patience
- Penetration
- Support
- Cover
- Angles
- Quick ball movement

Two Pitch Transition

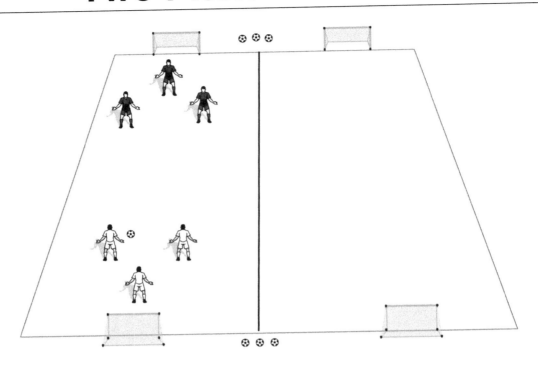

A normal 3v3 game. When a goal is scored, the team restarting play has the option to pass to the other pitch. Once the ball has gone onto that pitch, all players need to go onto the other pitch.

Progression 1

Any time the ball goes out of play, the pass can be switched onto the other pitch. Again, all players must switch pitches.

Progression 2

At any time, a pass can go onto the other pitch. All players switch pitches.

Progression 3

At any time, players can dribble onto the other pitch. All players switch pitches.

Progression 4

A goal cannot be scored until all teammates have switched pitches.

Points

- Awareness
- Understanding space
- Width
- Communication

Transfer/Transition

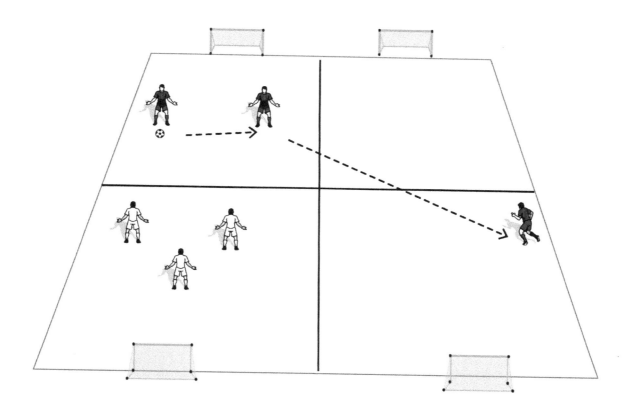

The play starts with a 2v3 attack on the left-hand pitch. On the right-hand pitch is a spare striped player. Once the ball is played across to the right, the players need to decide whether they should all follow, or whether only specific players should follow. Stripes leave one of their players spare on the left-hand pitch. Stripes can only score in the opposition half. If whites win the ball, they counter-attack.

Challenge for the spare player: should he or she drop into their half for an easy pass, or stay higher for a more difficult pass but an easier scoring chance?

Progression 1

Introduce the offside rule.

Progression 2

If play is switched, the stripes can send all of their players across, but the whites can only send two. How does this change supporting movement and positioning? How does this change the way the whites counter-attack?

Transition/Check

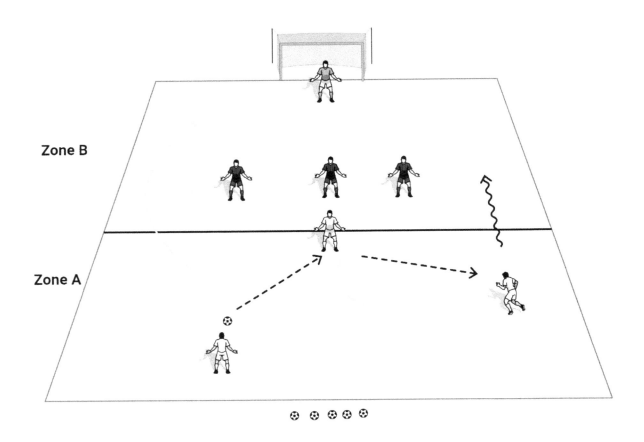

Zone B

Zone A

3v3 + Goalkeepers.

The white team attacks the striped team.

The attacking team can score from anywhere.

Both teams attack the same goal, but can only score if they have entered zone A. Thus, if the stripes win the ball in zone B, they need to move into zone A before they can shoot. The white team then needs to quickly get into a defensive position. If the stripes win the ball in zone A, they can attack immediately.

If a team scores, they attack again using one of the balls at the top of zone A.

What options do the teams have for defending?

How can they attack quickly when they win the ball?

How can the attacking team disorganise the defenders?

Real World

While transition topics are important tactically, one of their biggest plus points is that they are of a higher tempo than other practices. Transition-based games are great for lifting the intensity of groups who may lack this in their sessions.

Not only that, but they are fantastic for pre-season.

We often witness pre-season that is built around running and very little ball work. Slamming pre-season sessions is all the rage on social media in the summer months. Using transition-based games (and small-sided games in general) is a good way to get players working at a high tempo and fit for football. If we consider that by making the areas larger, we are giving the players a higher physical load, then transition sessions will help get players ready for the season and add the bonus that they will have high levels of ball contact while doing it.

9

Can our Session Plan be to Have No Session Plan?

The chapter title is clearly a paradoxical and contrarian notion. Yet, if our objective is to meet the needs of our players, there is every chance that they will have a good idea of what they need.

The more aware players are – of what they need to learn – the more likely they are to be good learners. If they can become aware of how they might learn, they may become even better learners. The only way for this to have a chance of happening is to cede some element of control to the players. This can be very hard for coaches, as it often runs contrary to what we have been told coaching actually is. To instruct, to cajole, to impose. Creating forms of the game that 'direct' learning is often acceptable to coaches, but to cede control can be a step too far.

What if the coach provides direction, but not instruction? The coach and the players collaborate in the process, with the coach steering the ship, but not forcing it in a specific direction.

If players can be entrusted with greater control, and become able to guide their own decision-making, they will become less reliant on the coach for direction. My goal is to be unnecessary. The players should not need me; they should be able to lead themselves. The process begins with stepping back and trusting the players.

This means that the coach needs to be prepared to be flexible. To do this as seamlessly as possible, we need an equally flexible area.

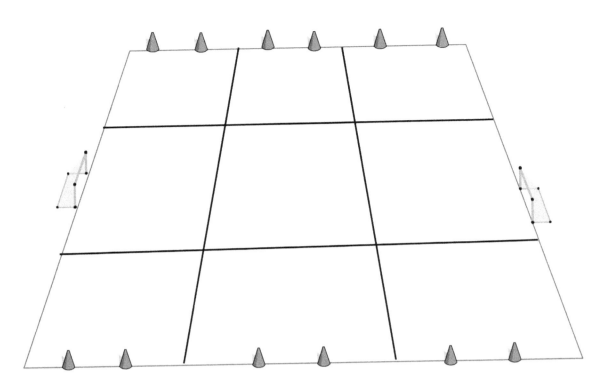

The above area is designed to provide different setups,
simply by moving a few cones.

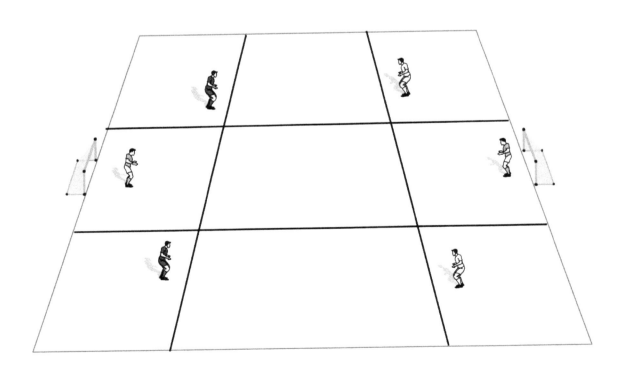

3v3 with zones

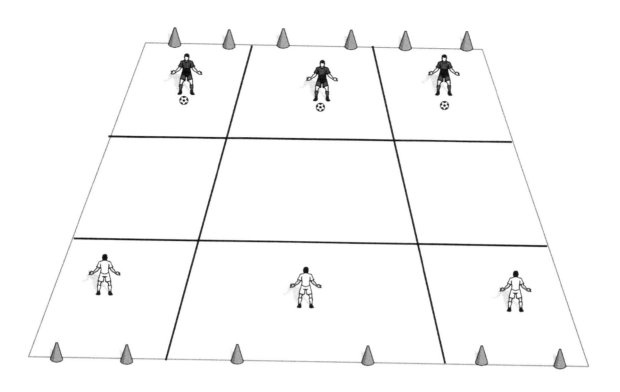

3x1v1

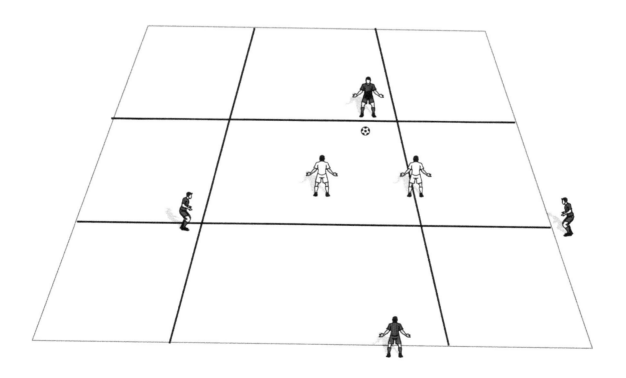

Rondo

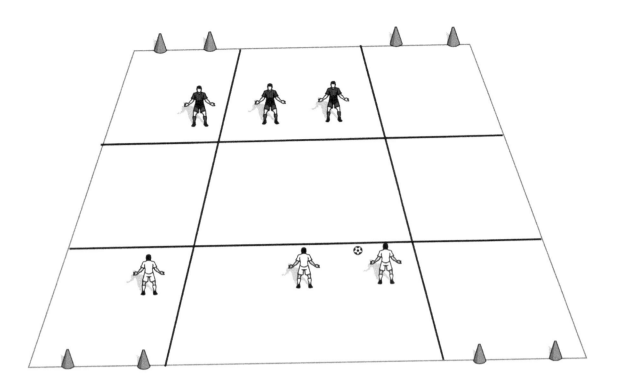

Four-goal game

Offset goals

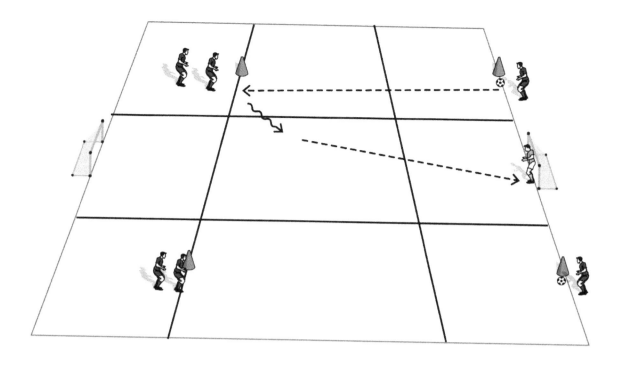

Shooting

Once we have an area that can handle most imaginable scenarios, we need a means by which to generate the session content. As coaches, we can come in with a general topic (e.g. passing), which the players may have played a role in generating.

An effective method for generating session content from a match is the use of questions designed to explore the game. Asking the players will also help establish their knowledge of the game, themselves, and each other. The term "checking for understanding" has often been used in coaching (although it has not always been clear how that happens in practice). As coaches, we might assume that we know players' levels of understanding, especially for those we have worked with over a period of time. Handing the players regular opportunities to show us what they understand replaces assumptions with knowledge.

Explore

Creativity and Imagination

- What is creativity?

- Are some players more creative than others? In what ways? Why might this be?

- Where and when will creativity be most useful? Can it be useful elsewhere?

- Are there limits on creativity?

- Which emotions would you attach to creativity? How does it make you feel?

Passing and Possession

- Why do we pass the ball?

- Are there different types of pass? How many types can we do? Why choose one type and not the other?

- Which parts of the foot can we pass with? Do we only use our feet to pass? What other parts of the body can we use?

- What makes a pass good? What makes a pass bad?

- What is possession? Why do we want it? Why might we not want it?

- What can the player with the ball do to help keep possession? What can the players without the ball do to help keep possession?

Space and Movement

- What is space? Where is the space?

- How do we know where the space is?

- Why do we want space?

- How much space do we need?

- How can we find the space? What is stopping you from finding space?

- What movement(s) can help you find space?

Dribbling and Running with The Ball

- Are there differences between dribbling and running with the ball?

- Why would we dribble? Why would we not dribble?

- Do we need to change direction when dribbling? Why? How?

- How many parts of the foot can we use to dribble? Why would it be better or worse to only use one foot while dribbling?

- How many different dribbling moves do we know? Can we come up with some new ones?

Control and Heading

- What do we mean by control? Why do we need it?

- Which parts of the body can use to control the ball?

- How do we decide which part of the body we use when we control the ball?

- Is there a difference between attacking headers and defensive headers?

- Do we have to jump to head the ball? How do we know?

- How can we head the ball with power? Why would we want to do this?

Shooting and Goalscoring

- How many ways can we think of to score a goal?

- Where are we aiming when we are trying to score? Which part of the goal gives us the best chance to score?

- Do we always shoot with power? Why? Which players can impact our choice of shot?

- How many touches might we need before shooting?

Leadership and Communication

- What is a good leader? Are you a good leader? How do you know?

- Which footballers have been good leaders? Does a player need to be captain to be a leader?

- Does a team need more than one leader? Why?

- What might communication be? What things do we need to communicate to our teammates? Is communication more important for certain positions?

- Are there football phrases that you know? What do they mean? How might we use them?

It is of vital importance to use open, divergent questions to enable the opportunity for players to develop and generate differing scenarios. If closed, convergent questions are used, the possible outcomes are far more limited as convergent questions tend to have a specific correct answer, while divergent questions will have multiple usable answers. Beginning questions with "How might" or "Describe to me" will produce more possible responses. We may begin with a convergent question to emphasise the topic, but quickly follow it up with divergent questioning.

"What is space?"

"How might we know where space is?"

The answers that players provide can then help to structure the practice. Using the area designed the grid system will help to identify space. Using the four-goal game, we might add a further influence on where space is, as would playing with offset goals. Players may also provide other answers to which these solutions are not relevant. The coach needs to be open enough to enable their suggestions.

The goal is to get the players thinking.

Pick your 5-a-side Team

You must have a goalkeeper

You can have one or two defenders

You can have one or two midfielders

You can have one or two forwards

- Do you choose your shape to fit your players, or your players to fit your shape? Why?
- You may pick from any players in the world (apart from Messi and Ronaldo). Who do you choose? Why?
- You may pick any players from the past or present.
- Pick your team made up of – Fictional characters – Animals – Musicians – Artists – Politicians – Vehicles – Wrestlers – or any other category(!) – Always think about why?

Which of these players or positions best suits your teammates?

Which one are you?

Which one do you want to be?

- (Add as appropriate)
-
-
-

By selecting their own 5-a-side team (or a format relevant to them), players are engaging in divergent thinking. Players may just select their favourite players, but by following a few rules, the players will have to think about who they are selecting and why? What qualities are they admiring in those players? Why are those qualities of use, particularly for the positions selected?

When asking them to select non-footballers, in positions, we are asking them to consider transferable qualities from other sports and different walks of life into football. Once they are asked to select which players in their team possess attributes – to fill the roles – they are displaying understanding of their teammates and themselves. They may decide to attempt to replicate the qualities in their performances, potentially developing new skills.

Using logical questions will be effective, but abstract ones can also prove powerful. Questions are brilliant for setting an early tone and creating a focus. The risk is that making the questions too abstract will cause 'buy out', so coaches have to judge the questions they use or be ready to justify their use of such questions in a convincing manner. The list below contains many examples that were created on the advice of artists, writers, and musicians. The list is by no means exhaustive.

Creative Questions

- Is creativity fun?
- What would happen if we use a different shape/size of ball? (Rugby ball, tennis ball, etc.)
- If football had no rules, what rules would you come up with?
- If you could remove any rule from football, what would it be? Why?
- If you could change the rules of the game, what would you change? (For example, every foul is a penalty. No walls allowed at free kicks.)
- Think of the most boring game of football. How can you make sure you never play in a game that boring?
- How can you make sure your team concedes a lot of goals?
- What would you do so that you never scored a goal ever again?
- What could you do that means your team never wins a game?
- What would make all of your passes bad?
- How could you make sure your shot didn't go in?
- What would happen if the pitch was a different shape?
- How would you play if the pitch had more than two goals on it?
- What would it be like if you played football on the moon? (Think of other locations/places.)
- What is the best way to injure yourself? How can you injure others?
- How many different places on the pitch can you score a goal from? What type of goal?
- How could you score a goal if you weren't allowed to – pass – dribble – shoot?
- What formation will get you goals? Why?
- What formation will concede goals? Why?
- What formation will control the midfield? Why?
- How can you keep the ball away from the other team? Why would you want to do this?
- What can happen if you LET the other team have the ball? How can this help your team win?
- What would happen if you could only walk/hop/skip/sidestep?
- What if you could not speak? What if you had to speak constantly? What would you say?
- You have to give the decisions against your team. Concede a penalty if you are caught cheating.
- If you could pick any non-football character to be your coach, who would you pick? Why?

- What would happen to the game if there were areas that you are not allowed into? It's a free kick to the opposition if you enter.
- Would football be a different game if no one ever watched?
- What makes for a boring practice? How can we avoid this?

The answers to the questions will both be positive and negative, but the effect of not being able to perform an action emphasises what is required *in order to* perform said action. For instance, in answer to the question, "What formation will concede goals?" the answer will likely involve playing no defenders or no central defenders. Thus, players know that when they pick a team, they need to have defenders. By twisting the game into barely recognisable shapes, we recognise the parts that are missing – deepening our understanding of the game and identifying the areas that have the potential to be developed.

Open-minded coaches will help players to be open-minded, helping forge the future of football. Football of 30 years ago looks very different to now, the goalkeeper could pick up back-passes and throw-ins, and the ball had to leave the area on goal kicks before it could be played again. We now have goal-line technology and VAR! The rules are constantly evolving; players and coaches should be too.

Real World

One day, at training, I came in with a few packs of a very popular brand of trading card that features famous footballers. The under-8s were so excited. We had four teams of three, and each team received an unopened pack. The challenge was to form a team using the players in the pack, and then explain why they had chosen those players. The next step was to work out which player each of them would try to replicate, if they could.

Players started trading cards because the balance wasn't right, or they needed a goalkeeper, or the player just didn't fit with their own attributes. The under-8s were showing an understanding of themselves, of each other, and of how to work as a team.

We took this into the next set of fixtures. The players had the full set of trading cards and chose a team based on both the cards and our players. Sometimes, the player would need to try and replicate the card (Zaha, for example); at other times, the card was chosen because it suited the role and one of our players (Luke Shaw was a great example of that). Team selection and the explanation of roles and responsibilities had been taken out of my hands, quite possibly for the better of the youngsters' long-term development.

Other Books from Bennion Kearny

The original book from Peter Prickett.

In this book, coaches of all levels, working with players across all age groups and abilities, will learn to utilise the 3v3 method to develop skilful individuals and effective teams. The book builds up from 1v1 to 3v3 through technical exercises that improve individual skills. Then, it moves beyond 3v3, adding in more players (including goalkeepers), as situations demand it.

With a core 3v3 training foundation, players will be able to explore and cement numerous key parts to their games, with depth and width, unlocking the various combinations – such as overlaps, one-twos, third-man runs, and more – which are used at all levels of the sport. At the same time, players will have ample opportunities to develop and perfect creative dribbling moves.

Developing Skill: A Guide to 3v3 Soccer Coaching outlines how you can use and incorporate the 3v3 method in your training and provides more than 90 ready-to-use, illustrated practices. It also details how best to run warm-ups, how to work with different pitch sizes and shapes, and much more.

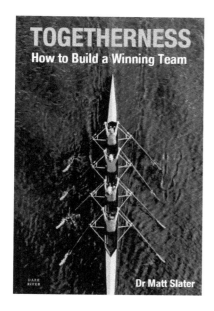

TOGETHERNESS
How to Build a Winning Team

DARK RIVER

Dr Matt Slater

DARK RIVER

Vasilis Papadakis

Pre-Season Soccer Training

A Seven Week, 50 Session Guide to Building For The New Season

DARK RIVER

"A must-have for all referees"
Keith Hackett

BLOWING THE WHISTLE
The Psychology of Football Refereeing

STUART CARRINGTON

BENNION KEARNY

GARY CURNEEN

THE MODERN SOCCER COACH
3-IN-1

A FOUR DIMENSIONAL APPROACH | POSITION-SPECIFIC TRAINING | PRE-SEASON TRAINING

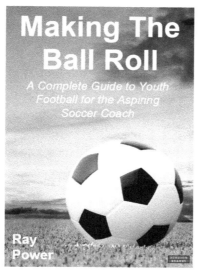

Making The Ball Roll

A Complete Guide to Youth Football for the Aspiring Soccer Coach

Ray Power

BENNION KEARNY

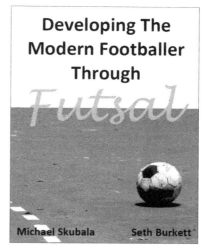

Developing The Modern Footballer Through

Futsal

Michael Skubala   Seth Burkett

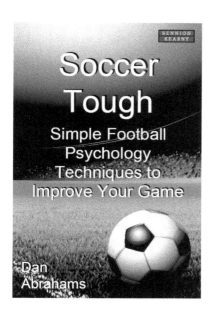

BENNION KEARNY

Soccer Tough

Simple Football Psychology Techniques to Improve Your Game

Dan Abrahams

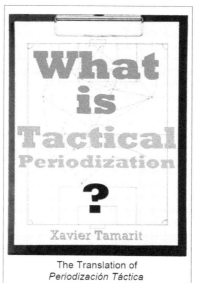

What is Tactical Periodization

?

Xavier Tamarit

The Translation of
Periodización Táctica

Confidence Commitment
Control 5Cs Communication

Coaching Psychological Skills in Youth Football
Developing The 5Cs

Chris Harwood
Richard Anderson

BENNION KEARNY

Deliberate Soccer Practice

50 Defending Football Exercises to Improve Decision-Making

Ray Power

101 GOALKEEPER TRAINING PRACTICES

> Warm-Ups
> Individual GK Practices
> Small GK Group Practices
> Team-Based Practices

ANDY ELLERAY

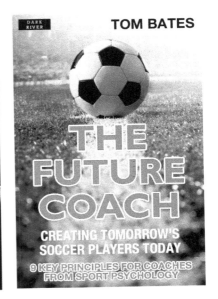

TOM BATES

THE FUTURE COACH

CREATING TOMORROW'S SOCCER PLAYERS TODAY

9 KEY PRINCIPLES FOR COACHES FROM SPORT PSYCHOLOGY

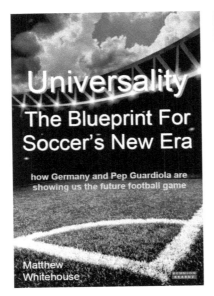

Universality

The Blueprint For Soccer's New Era

how Germany and Pep Guardiola are showing us the future football game

Matthew Whitehouse

PLAY LIKE PEP GUARDIOLA'S BARCELONA

A Soccer Coach's Guide

Agustín Peraita

The English translation of the Spanish bestseller "Quiero que mi equipo juegue como el F.C.Barcelona de Guardiola"

Foreword by Ray Power

Paul Webb Academy

Strength Training for Footballers

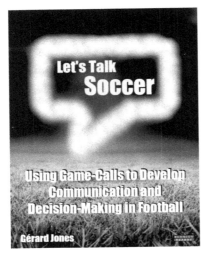

Let's Talk Soccer

Using Game-Calls to Develop Communication and Decision-Making in Football

Gérard Jones

SOCCER TRAINING BLUEPRINTS

15 Ready-to-Run Sessions for Outstanding Attacking Play

James Jordan

DEVELOPING SOCCER PLAYERS FORWARD-SPECIFIC PRACTICES
DAN BOLAS